FEARFULLY

and

Wonderfully

W*ei*RD

Other wonderful, fine Door Books:

The Adventures of Brother Biddle
The Door Interviews
Fearfully and Wonderfully Weird
101 Things to Do During a Dull Sermon

FEARFULLY

and

Wonderfully
W*ei*RD

A SCREWBALL LOOK AT
THE CHURCH AND OTHER THINGS
FROM THE PAGES OF

The Wittenburg Door

COMPILED BY DOUG PETERSON
AND DR. H. WINFIELD TUTTE, Ph.D., Th.D., M & M

The Door/Z

Zondervan Publishing House
Grand Rapids, Michigan

FEARFULLY AND WONDERFULLY WEIRD
Copyright © 1990 by Youth Specialties, Inc.
The Door Books, 1224 Greenfield Drive, El Cajon, California 92021, are published by
Zondervan Publishing House, 1415 Lake Drive, S.E., Grand Rapids, Michigan 49506

Library of Congress Cataloging-in-Publication Data
Fearfully and wonderfully weird / [edited] by Doug Peterson.
    p.   cm.
    Contains selections of humorous articles and cartoons from past issues of the
magazine Wittenburg door.
    ISBN 0-310-28731-6 : $10.95 (est.)
    1. American wit and humor. 2. Christianity—Humor. 3. American wit and
humor, Pictorial. 4. Christianity—Caricatures and cartoons. I. Peterson, Doug.
II. Wittenburg Door.
PN6231.C35F4 1990
818'.5407—dc20   90-32278
                                                    CIP

Edited and designed by Blue Water Ink

Printed in the United States of America

90 91 92 93 94 95 / CH / 10 9 8 7 6 5 4 3 2 1

You created my inmost being; you knit me together in my mother's womb. I praise you because I am fearfully and wonderfully made.

— David, Psalm 139:13–14

Angels can fly because they can take themselves lightly.

— G. K. Chesterton

A cow is smiling if its ears are tilted forward.

— H. Winfield Tutte

Contents

3

The Membrane That Connects Your Tongue to the Bottom of Your Mouth — *Communication*

News Briefs *by Doug Peterson* • Margin Notes • Amy Grant: "I Was Raised by Family of Wild Wolfhounds" *by Kraig Klaudt* • Dear Abbot *by Roy Rivenburg* • Truth Is Stranger Than Fiction • TV Guidepost *by Kraig Klaudt* • Mr. Accordian *by Dan Pegoda* • Art and Satire: The Door Mini-Interview with Dan Pegoda • Dear Chicken

4

Arms That Have No Feeling When You Wake Up Because You Slept on Them Wrong — *Church Life*

Performance Appraisal for Church Youth Workers *by Kathryn Lindskoog* • A New Proposal for the Church Year *by LeRoy Koopman* • As the Pulpit Turns *by Doug Peterson* • Truth Is Stranger Than Fiction • The Forgotten Addiction *by James F. Sennett* • A Young Man Approaches a Woman Seated Behind a Desk *by Dinah Stokes* • The Wittenburg Dare! • Some Good Ol' American Memory Verses *by Den Hart* • Margin Notes

5

The Hollow Part on the Inside of Your Leg Right Behind the Knee — *Social and Political Issues*

Ground Zero: Wheaton *by Kraig Klaudt* • Sobouring • Psalm 2023 *by Erik C. Nelson* • Cold War *by Kraig Klaudt* • Hazards and Hot Water *by William H. Willimon* • The Heart of Racism *by Jean Caffey Lyles* • Truth Is Stranger Than Fiction • A Feminine Faith *by Ben Patterson* • Macho Feminism *by Jean Caffey Lyles* • Truth Is Stranger Than Fiction • Margin Notes

Introduction, Foreword, Preface, and Introduction to the Preface

I decided to lump all these things together because who reads them anyway? I'll just get them all out of the way with one little section because probably the only people reading this are my mother and maybe my wife. My five-year-old will probably draw pictures on this page of Teenage Mutant Ninja Turtles playing volleyball with Mister Rogers.

I bet I could use this introduction to write the most controversial, shocking things ever to appear in print, and I wouldn't even get one nasty letter complaining about it. In fact, I think I'm going to do it right now. I'm going to write something unbelievably shocking, and the Zondervan Publishing Company probably won't even notice because I bet even my editor skips this introduction. So get ready. Here goes. I'm going to do it. I really am. You just wait. I'm going to say something very sensational and amazing and tantalizing and controversial and . . .

—by Doug Peterson
   and H. Winfield Tutte (who stopped him in the nick of time)
   January 20, 1990

Introduction

Foreword

Preface, and

Introduction to

the Preface

Fearfully and
Wonderfully
Weird

All parts of the body serve vital functions. But when people marvel about the human body, they tend to focus on the same old parts—the brain, the heart, the eyes, the mouth. When was the last time you heard somebody go bananas over that little indentation between your nose and your upper lip? And when was the last time you saw a *Reader's Digest* article entitled, "I Am Joe's Eyebrows That Connect in the Middle Over the Nose"?

This tendency to ignore strange parts of the body is common in popular science books. It's even common in religious books.

Since New Testament days, Christians have compared the human body to the body of Christ; some have even explained how specific organs in the body can teach us about how the church body functions. Although this is great, all of the publicity continues to go to the celebrity organs. To get all that publicity, those organs must spend half their time making media contacts. Our hearts would probably be a lot stronger if they spent less energy on public relations and more on obliterating the huge masses of Twinkie cream lumbering through our arteries.

To give a little more balance to our view of the body, this book looks at parts that never get attention. Odd parts of the human body. And odd parts of the church—the body of Christ. It does this by examining selected works from one of the oddest parts of the church, *The Wittenburg Door*—a magazine that has a lot in common with a toothache.

The Wittenburg Door started in 1969 as a four-page mimeographed publication distributed to Southern California youth workers, as well as to one or two people related to the editors and two dozen people who soon began denying they were related to the editors. The publication borrowed its name from the church door in Wittenberg, Germany, where Martin Luther posted his famous 95 Theses, the document that began the Reformation.

In 1971, *The Wittenburg Door* switched hands and became an official magazine, complete with its misspelled name. In the first issue, "Witten*berg*" was spelled "Witten*burg*." Thanks to the thorough seminary training of the staff, nobody noticed, and the misspelled name remained. Then, in 1989, the magazine became known simply as *The Door*. It even began to be printed on slick paper, and it included only a few misspellings per issue rather than the usual two dozen.

One thing hasn't changed, however: the magazine's goal, which is to help the church laugh at itself. The church can get into big trouble when it takes itself too seriously. As former *Door* editor Ben Patterson once put it, the church is a mixture of things that are "of God" and things that are "of man." The danger comes when we start thinking that *everything* in the church comes from God. Learning to laugh at ourselves when we foolishly confuse the two is a good remedy for that error.

All bodies have flaws (if you're in doubt, go put on a pair of leotards), and the church is no exception. Like other parts of the church body, *The Door* has its share of imperfections. But all parts of the body, even the odd and the flawed ones, have something to teach us.

1

Dandruff and Dead Skin

Flaky Things

A salesman once tried to sell me a vacuum cleaner by describing in great detail the amount of dead cells that crumble off my head every day, filling my house—a million bits of dead hair and skin that need to be cleaned up. He made it sound so bad, I wondered if executioners through the ages could have avoided a lot of blood and gore if they had just put their condemned prisoners in the guillotine and waited for their heads to flake off as tiny pieces of dead skin.

The salesman wasn't entirely off-base, though. I have heard that the skin on our head crumbles off and regenerates itself every month. So flakiness is a very natural, normal part of life. And it's a good place to begin our exploration of weird parts of the church body, because *The Door* ranks as one of the flakiest things around. (No, I didn't say the rankest, I said the flakiest.)

What other publication comes out with such irregularity that its Christmas issue appears in July? Of course, there are always good reasons for coming out months behind schedule. Take Issue #66, for instance, in which an editor's memo on the second page explained why the April/May issue had come out in October:

"First of all, everything would have been fine if April and May hadn't come so early this year. If that wasn't bad enough, when the original copy for the April/May issue was mailed to our secretary,

Judy, it was blown up in the mailbox by what the police now believe was a *Moody Monthly* terrorist group.

"The articles were re-typed and delivered by armed Amway salesmen to our artist. As Dan laid the articles out, he was injured by a freak accident. A berserk devotee of Robert Schuller crashed through the door of Dan's office and hit him over the head with a stack of Robert Schuller's books. After Dan recovered from his concussion in August, he finally was ready to send the April/May issue to the printer. Then the real tragedy struck.

"The art work was accidentally sent to Oral Roberts University where Richard Roberts laid hands on the art work and healed it. The issue immediately became *Christianity Today*. Finally, we were able to re-type and re-do the art work and finish this April/May issue in October, so here it is."

If that's not flaky enough, then let's talk about typographical errors. It's been estimated that there are more typographical errors in an average issue of *The Door* than there is dead skin in my house

every day. For example, in a 1983 interview, Ed Dobson's last name was consistently spelled "Dobbins." But, once again, there was a perfectly logical explanation. Fortunately, *The Door* had just installed voice-activated tape recorders in its offices in case something like this happened, so they have a recording of exactly what happened the day the "Dobbins" mistake was made. Here is a transcript:

EDITOR: Don, are you there?

DAN: This is Dan.

EDITOR: Oh, hi Dan. Is Don there?

DAN: My name is Dan, not Don.

EDITOR: I know that.

DAN: Well, what do you want?

EDITOR: Is the Dobbins interview laid out yet?

DAN: You mean the Dobson interview.

EDITOR: Did we interview James Dobson?

DAN: No, Ed Dobson. Ed Dobson.

EDITOR: Ed Dobson? I thought it was James Dobson.

DAN: Ed Dobson is a different person than James Dobson. They are two different people.

EDITOR: I know that, Don.

DAN: Dan!

EDITOR: Dan Dobson?

DAN: . . . .

EDITOR: Well, anyway, do you have the Ed Dobbins interview ready?

DAN: Whatever you say.

EDITOR: Thanks, Don.

DAN: Dan.

With all such things made perfectly clear, let's venture forth into a minefield of flaky things from past issues of *The Door*. And since we're really courageous, we'll take our first peek at some samples from the regular (whatever that means in *Door* order) "Truth Is Stranger Than Fiction" section—some of the flakiest true items you'll ever encounter.

"TOTALLY AWESOME"

[11]So there was this old dude who had two sons [12]The youngest one was like y'know a total babe, for sure. The older one was a total zod, like a real space cadet, totally. So this young dude is like freakin' out, like totally boared and stuff. There was nothing to do, like nothing. So he goes to his dad and says, "I'm sure, I'm going to stay here the rest of my life. Like gag me with a spoon. I mean barf me out. This place is totally gross, like grody to the max. I want like my share of your mega-bucks so I can like pig out on junk food and buy clothes, for sure." So his dad like gave him his share of the mega-bucks [13]and like this young babe went totally spaz. For sure. Like scarf and junk food and lowies to the max. And rolfing all night long. Like totally freaked out. I am so sure. Gag me.

The Valley Bible
T.M.

Have you ever wondered when somebody was going to put the awkward and formal wording of the Living Bible into a language today's generation can understand? Well, wonder no longer, cuz *The Valley Bible* is here! That's right. Weekends of extra-credit work by the Inner Vacancy chapter of California's Encino University has produced the definitive translation for the eighties. *The Valley Bible* preserves the accuracy of the Living Bible while eliminating ambiguous phrases like, "I don't believe you," or "that makes me upset." Like we're talking Bible to the max here, so pick up your copy today. For sure!

"Yeah, a really tubular Bible." — F. F. Bruce Jr.

"Like ya know, if you see only one movie a year make sure it's this one for sure."
— Karla Henry Jr.

From Issue #66/April–May, 1982

Another fine Wycliff product. No. 256 in a series of 700. Collect them all and trade them with your friends.

WHAT TO DO WITH THE BUSSES

WRITTEN AND COMPILED BY DOOR STAFF

WITH GAS PRICES THE WAY THEY ARE TODAY, ONE OF THE FIRST QUESTIONS BEING ASKED IS; "<u>WHAT ARE THEY GOING TO DO WITH THE CHURCH BUSSES?</u>" -- OR, TO PUT IT ANOTHER WAY; "<u>WHAT WILL HAPPEN TO THEM?</u>"... YES, THERE MANY WAYS TO ASK THIS QUESTION -- ALMOST AS MANY, WE BELIEVE, AS THERE ARE WAYS TO ANSWER IT. LET US ILLUSTRATE.

ADDED WINGS FOR EXTRA SEATING

BUSDOMINIUMS

PLUG UP A VOLCANO

SWIMMING BUS

BUS PACKING (AND AISLE EXPLORATION)

A PAPERWEIGHT

ABUSEMENT PARK

(Cartoons on pages 16–17 from issue #54/April–May, 1980)

PIÑATA

VBS CRAFTS (ELMER'S GLUE, MACARONI, SILVER SPRAY PAINT, BUS.)

SUNDAY SCHOOL PRIZES (ATTENDENCE BUSSES)

BUS HENGE

OFFERING BUS

B-plus for bee buses

PASCO, Wash. (AP)
—Russell Ferguson has to get a bee-plus in ingenuity.

The well-schooled farmer knows his alfalfa seed crops can't survive without pollenation from leaf cutter bees. So he bought a fleet of buses to keep the bees on board.

He purchased seven old white Sunday school buses formerly used by the Riverview Baptist Church in Pasco. In earlier days, the buses were painted yellow and served students in Mid-Columbia school districts.

Now the fleet is parked in Ferguson's field, about 10 miles north of Pasco. On one side of each bus, windows have been painted white to keep the bees from being fried by the summer sun. The other side of each bus, away from the prevailing winds, has been cut away so the bees can get on and off the buses easily.

Over the years, farmers have used boxes, lean-tos, small buildings and even old, doorless refrigerators to house their bees.

Old pickups equipped with small houses, trailers lined with boxes and even houses on skids have been employed. But nary a bus.

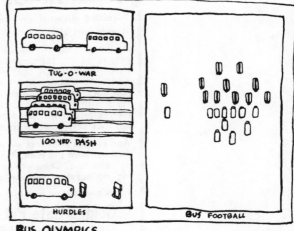

BUS OLYMPICS

TUG-O-WAR

100 YRD. DASH

HURDLES

BUS FOOTBALL

STORE NUCLEAR WASTE

(Cartoons on pages 18–19 from issue #56/August–September, 1980)

ABOVE: From Issue #43/June–July, 1978;
BELOW: From Issue #105/May–June, 1989.

Zany vicar plans a resurrection

By GLEN PERKINSON

Christchurch's zaniest man of the cloth intends to rise again on the third day.

The vicar of St Martins Anglican Church, the Rev Simon Ballantyne, has agreed to be buried 4m underground for two days in a garden shed in a fund-raising stunt for the church fair. He will disappear on Thursday, September 22, at 10 a.m. until the morning of Saturday, September 24.

This is the third stunt Mr Ballantyne has performed in the name of his church. In 1985 he was hoisted to the top of St Martins' church bell tower for 50 hours. In 1986 the church's fair committee put him on a raft in the Estuary.

He is not much concerned about his subterranean sojourn.

"It does not pose too many problems—I am not claustrophobic. I always find these things adventurous and intriguing," he said.

The shed will be buried on an empty section opposite the Waltham Arms Hotel in Waltham Road. Mr Ballantyne's only fear is if it should rain heavily before he emerges from his temporary underground home.

"The water-table is a worry if it rains like crazy because it could rise up. But we will deal with that if it happens."

He said he was happy with the safety procedures for his stunt and if the worst came to the worst "I'm sure a miracle would see me burst forth."

Mr Ballantyne's family have become "a little embarrassed" about his latest prank but have learned to take most things in their stride.

The 2.5m by 2m shed has been given by Skyline Garages. Mr Ballantyne will stock it with food and water and arrange for adequate ventilation and entertainment—a television, radio and ham radio set.

There will also be a telephone so that he can keep in contact with the higher world.

From Issue #56/August–September, 1980

In keeping a promise made to his congregation, Pastor George Y. Elliott of Rosedale Union Church ate dinner atop the church roof after Sunday school attendance reached 100.

Church Tries Credit

'Charge It' Becomes New Way to Tithe

HOUSTON (UPI) —A few members of Christ the King Lutheran Church raised their eyebrows at the prospect of tithing by credit card, but the Rev. Ed Peterman says the system is now being accepted by his parishioners.

"We believe the contributions will be made more promptly because people usually pay their credit card bills and then wonder if they have anything left over," Peterman said.

"Now, they can put their pledge on the credit card and pay it later."

He said there had been some initial fears that the move "might be considered too commercial," but he said the church decided last fall to give members a "third opportunity," in addition to cash or checks to make their donations.

Peterman said three credit card contributions were made on the first Sunday the system was used. Now it is being used regularly by many members, he said.

He said Texas Commerce Medical Bank designed special forms for the church to use. The forms can be dropped into the collection plate without the noisy use of a credit card machine.

The bank is giving the church a discount, charging 3% rather than the usual 5% for credit card transactions.

From Issue #69/ October–November, 1982

21

Truth Is Stranger Than Fiction

WILL CLIFF HAVE TO KISS A REAL PIG ?

Yes, if Sunday school attendance reaches 250 or more Sept. 7th at the Wasco Pentecostal Church of God, Cliff Wymer, the Assistant Superintendent will KISS A REAL PIG the following Sunday!

However; if attendance is 300 or more Steve Newton the Superintendent will join him!

Pastor Johnny Ross urges everyone who does not attend a Sunday School to begin Sept. 7th with 'I Believe in S.S.' (Sunday School).

S.S. Buttons will be given away and free transportation is provided within city limits

Simply call 758-6505

or 758-6240

S.S. Begins at 9:45 a.m. and is open to all ages

Come and bring your friends

WASCO PENTECOSTAL CHURCH OF GOD
POSO & ADAMS

ABOVE: From Issue #57/October–November, 1980
BELOW: From Issue #76/December, 1983–January, 1984

YOUR YARD CAN LOOK LIKE THIS!

T.P. DECORATING, INC.
INTERIORS **EXTERIORS**
"YOU NAME IT, WE DECORATE IT!"
HOMES, BUSINESS, SCHOOLS, CHURCHES
FOR FREE ESTIMATE, SEE CASEY GWINN, COLLEGE AND CAREER CLASS, 9:00 A.M. SUN.
PLYMOUTH CONGREGATIONAL CHURCH
12058 BEVERLY, WHITTIER, CALIF. 90601

WHAT'S BLACK AND WHITE AND READ ALL OVER?

You Guessed It...

The Wittenburg Door Study Bible

And we mean "ALL over." Our unique new edition of the sacred book stands more than 17' high, by 14' wide. You might ask, "Why so big?" Well, having noticed the current trend in Bible Publishing—one edition with this "special feature," another with that "added help," and still others with you name it—we said to ourselves, "This is silly. What we need is another Study Bible. One with everything we can possibly think of in it!"

WEATHER RESISTANT COVER

OVER 8,000,000 PAGES

ACTUAL TYPE SIZE

NOAH'S ARCH ILLUSTRATIONS

SIZE IN PROPORTION TO A FARMER

SPECIFICATIONS: 17'3" x 14' x 5'2". WEIGHT: 4,295 lbs

EVERYTHING WE COULD POSSIBLY THINK OF TO PUT IN IT:

- **Early Hebrew Texts**
- **Early Greek Texts**
- **Original Proof Texts**
- **Original Chinese Translation**
- **All Other Translations** (including the CB Lingo Version and Official C.I.A. Coded Version for even more challenge in your study.)
- **Concordance** (and other dance diagrams)
- **Parallel Comparisons**
- **Diagonal Footnotes**
- **Horizontal Words** (for easy reading)
- **Special Cross References to:**
  - —Entire Wittenburg Door Library
  - —Chronicles of Narnia
  - —Guinness Book of World Records
  - —Way Out, Right On, and Far Out Ideas for Youth Groups
  - —Mike Warnke
  - **ALL INCLUDED!**
- **Table of Weights and Measurements**
- **Table of Contents** (complete with discussion guide)
- **Table**
- **Maps of Holy Land:** Jerusalem, Wheaton, El Cajon
- **Sing-a-longs** (including lyrics to "Do the Concor")
- **Commentaries by Dr. H. Winfield Tutte** (like, "YOWSA")
- **Shakespeare's Complete Works**
- **Shakespeare's Incomplete Works**
- **Illustrations, Diagrams, Charts, Timelines, Page Numbers**
- **Reproductions of Famous Masters' Biblical Paintings** (original sizes)
- **Our Favorite Verses Color Coordinated** (1 Chron. 26:18, for instance, would be printed in the same color as a Parbar.)

PLUS THESE NOTABLE FEATURES!

- Sturdy Press Board Cover: upholstered in attractive LEATHER-LOOK' vinyl.
- Compartments, Shelves: built right into inside cover (for adding anything we might've forgotten)
- Brushes, Rollers and Paint: for hi-lighting, underlining.
- Predog-eared Pages: give that serious Bible reader look
- Fold-out Chairs: for discussion groups
- Ladder (doubles as book mark)
- Tape and Record Library: supplement your reading with great music and speakers (Bach, Vivaldi, Luther, Campolo, Schaeffer, Sinatra, Martin, Cosby, Peaches and Herb)
- Costume Closet: enjoy your favorite passages in the garb of the day.
- Walk Thru the Bible: easy to follow steps for literally hiking through Old and New Testaments.
- "Pop-Up" Designs: including tents to accommodate longer walks.
- Handy Car Trailer: for easy toting to church and meetings.
- An Accordian

AND WE'VE ONLY MENTIONED THE HIGHLIGHTS!

"It's a big book."
—Pat Boone

"I practically got lost in it!"
—Debbie Boone

"Never heard of it."
—Daniel Boone

"Sheeeesh!" —Elma Dowdings
1226 Greenfield Dr.
(Our neighbor)

Inerrant, Infallible, Incomprehensible!

Just think what an influence the W.D. Study Bible could be upon your friends and neighbors (or anyone else it might happen to be upon). You'll be able to hold studies in the book of Romans IN the book of Romans! There will be no more leaving the Bible on the shelf, or in the house, for that matter. Great for reference (can be seen for blocks!)... Great for studies (without ceilings!) ... Great for families (three or four at once!)

THIS IS A LIMITED EDITION, SO ACT NOW!

Actually we've only made one of these babies, and we're not real sure what to charge ... how does $10,000.95 sound?

From Issue #52/February–March, 1980

EL FOLDO CH

El Foldo in closed position. Note unique trailer hitch which can be attached to any car simply by ramming through trunk lid.

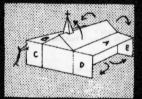

To unfold, swing roof panels "A" and "B" out. Swing wall section "C" through "F" into position. Raise steeple and cross.

Next swing walls "G" and "H" down. Slide floor sections into place. Rebuild right side which collapsed under weight.

You are done! Congratulations!

Light fixture doubles as collection plate

Both men and women's facilities provided just like a real church!

Sinks double as collection plates

Choir loft folds out like accordion (organ underneath)

Razor sharp rear bumper cuts down trees and other obstructions for easy parking in remote areas

Taillights designed to look like stained-glass windows

Note: An econ
Space is

24

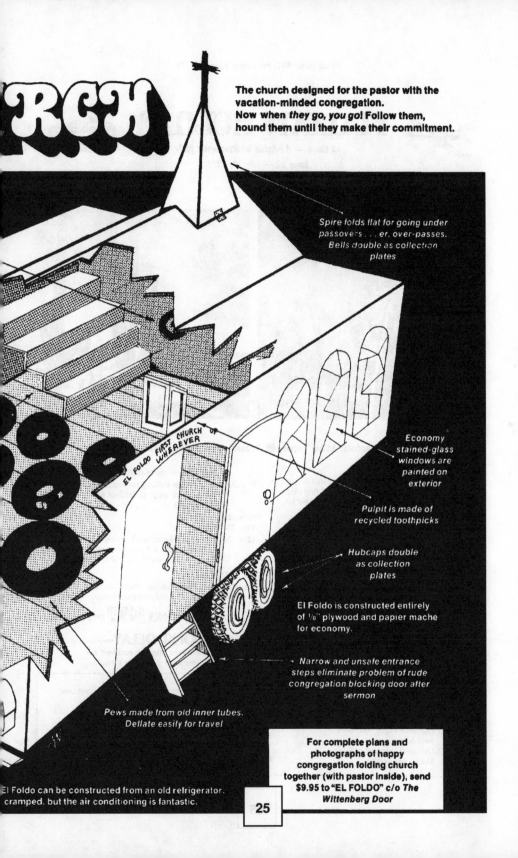

RCH

The church designed for the pastor with the vacation-minded congregation.
Now when *they go, you go!* Follow them, hound them until they make their commitment.

Spire folds flat for going under passovers . . . er, over-passes. Bells double as collection plates

EL FOLDO FIRST CHURCH OF WHEREVER

Economy stained-glass windows are painted on exterior

Pulpit is made of recycled toothpicks

Hubcaps double as collection plates

El Foldo is constructed entirely of ⅛" plywood and papier mache for economy.

Narrow and unsafe entrance steps eliminate problem of rude congregation blocking door after sermon

Pews made from old inner tubes. Deflate easily for travel

El Foldo can be constructed from an old refrigerator. cramped, but the air conditioning is fantastic.

ITALIAN HOLIDAY

12 Days — 4 Nights in Romantic Italy
June 22 — July 31, 1978

Tour Directors: Mike Yaconelli, Wayne Rico, Denny Rydbergoni

ITINERARY:

1st. Day Leave San Francisco International Airport at 4:35 A.M. All passengers travel first class aboard Italia Air's Uni-Engine Jumbo Jet.

2nd. Day In air.

3rd. Day In air.

4th. Day In air.

5th. Day Arrive Rome 9:00 P.M. and on to Rome Hilton Basement Annex for box dinner.

6th. Day After breakfast, complete city tour of Rome, 9:30-9:40 A.M. Free time for shoplifting followed by a fabulous 7-course meal (a salami and a six pack).

7th. Day Tour the countryside in the comfort of a rebuilt Italian Army Tank. Some continue on by jeep to Sicily (optional).

8th. Day Back in Rome for a tour of the University of Italy (both buildings). Everyone will get to see the book in the Health Science Library.

9th. Day Board your waiting Jumbo Jet to U.S.A. only three quick stops (2 for fuel and 1 for directions).

10th. Day In air.

11th. Day In air.

12th. Day Arrive San Francisco International Airport between 10:00 A.M. and midnight, depending on weather conditions and fuel leakage.

INCLUDES ALL

Transportation, meals, drugs, tours, transfers, hotel accommodations, first aid and parachutes.

• • • • • • ONLY $49.⁵⁰ per couple

DON'T DELAY—
Reservations must be received no later than departure time.

☐ Please reserve _____ places on the "TRIP TO ITALY". Enclosed is my check for $2.98 deposit (not returnable).

Please check:

    ☐ Optional Flight Insurance $400.00 per person.

    ☐ Optional side trip to Sicily $12.50 per person.

NAME_____

ADDRESS _____

NEXT OF KIN _____

BLOOD TYPE _____

26

TIRED OF A DOMINEERING HUSBAND?

THEN YOU NEED

AEROBIC AGGRESSION!©

Many people believe the Bible says that women should not exercise authority over men (we know better, of course), but one thing is for sure — nowhere does the Bible prohibit women from exercising over men. Therefore, we urge women to take our 15-week course in **AEROBIC AGGRESSION!**© In these easy-to-follow lessons, we will teach you how to exercise on your man and put an end to any of his domineering tendencies.

Here is what one Wisconsin woman said about our course:

"I've been exercising over my husband for a year and it has turned my marriage around! My husband used to dominate our household so much that I even had to get his OK before I sneezed. But I signed up for the **AEROBIC AGGRESSION!**© course and now my husband is a changed man! Every morning for the past year, I did 50 jumping jacks on his back, 40 wind sprints along his spine, 20 push-ups on his face, and 10 minutes of jogging on his ankles. After that kind of workout, my husband was in no shape to dominate me for the rest of the day!"

AEROBIC AGGRESSSION!© is recommended by Dr. Dobson-Scanzoni, author of *Focus On The Female* and *Blame It On Your Hormones.*

To register for this 15-week course, write to: **AEROBIC AGGRESSION!**© **Box 516, Adamsville, Rhode Island 56721.** Send $150 and we will give you two **AEROBIC AGGRESSION!**© albums, a full-color study guide, three exercise charts, and a first-aid kit.

From Issue #72/April–May, 1983

By Dan Pegoda
From Issue #57/
October–November, 1980

2

The Itchy Spot You Cannot Reach in the Middle of Your Back

Outreach

Clifford Ray, a former basketball star for the Golden State Warriors, was once asked to stick his arm into the stomach of a 350-pound dolphin and pull out a piece of metal. According to John May's book *Curious Facts*, Clifford's three-foot, nine-inch arms qualified him for the job.

But I bet that even Clifford Ray has trouble reaching that mysterious itchy spot in the middle of his back.

We all fall short in our attempts to reach particularly annoying itches, just as we all fall short in our attempts to reach out to others—whether it's with financial, emotional,

or spiritual support. But that doesn't mean we shouldn't try. It simply means we should understand our limitations, as my friend Bob Husband learned through experience.

Bob once struck up a conversation in an airport restaurant with a guy carrying a guitar. After a few minutes of casual chatter the guy suddenly said, "You know, there are a lot of lonely people out there."

Bob perked up. *All right, Lord, do you want me to tell this guy about you?* he wondered. So he asked, "What do you think causes them to be lonely?"

Without hesitation, the guy

answered adamantly, "It's because they don't know Jesus." And for the next fifteen minutes he preached at Bob, evidently assuming he was a pagan junior executive. By the time Bob was able to get a word in, he decided it would be too embarrassing to tell the guy he was already a Christian. So my friend played along.

As he said farewell, the guy took a handful of Jesus newspapers out of his guitar case, gave them to Bob, and told him they'd help him find the truth.

Bob boarded his plane thinking about how incredibly insensitive the guy was. To prove to himself how much better he was at reaching out with the Gospel, he decided to use the Jesus newspapers to minister to the person sitting next to him on the plane.

Rather than preach in the man's face, Bob opened one of the newspapers and hoped his seatmate would notice it and initiate a conversation. Nothing happened, so Bob held the newspaper further out, almost at arm's length. Nothing happened. He subtly moved it in the man's direction. Still noth-

ing happened. He rattled the newspaper.

Bob was about to give up on his witnessing plan when the stewardess came by. "Mr. Nelson," she said to the passenger next to him, "just stay seated when we reach Cleveland and I'll come back and help you off the plane."

That's when Bob realized the man in the window seat was blind. At the same time Bob realized that his ability to reach out was as in limited as that of the man in the airport.

Through the years *The Door* has looked at some of the ways we try to reach out to people. This chapter reviews a variety of them—evangelism, missions, ministry to the poor, and healings. Hopefully it will keep us humble as it shows us how far short we fall when we try to reach the itch.

But don't worry. Even when we botch things up royally and are embarrassed by our limitations, God still works in people's lives. When our arms aren't quite long enough, his are.

They're even longer than Clifford Ray's.

THE PIT

By Kenn Filkins

From Issue #96, April/May, 1987

A man fell into a pit and couldn't get himself out.

A SUBJECTIVE person came along and said:

"I FEEL for you, down there."

An OBJECTIVE person said:

"It's logical that someone would fall down there."

A CHRISTIAN SCIENTIST came along:

"You only THINK that you are in a pit."

A PHARISEE said:

"Only BAD people fall into a pit."

A MATHEMATICIAN calculated HOW he fell into the pit.

A ROCK-HOUND asked him of any rare specimens in the pit.

A NEWS REPORTER wanted the exclusive story on his pit.

A FUNDAMENTALIST said:

"You DESERVE your pit."

CONFUCIUS said:

"If you would have listened to me, you would not be in that pit."

BUDDHA said:

"Your pit is only a state of mind."

A REALIST said:

"That's a pit."

A SCIENTIST calculated the pressure necessary (lbs./sq.in.) to get him out of the pit.

A GEOLOGIST told him to appreciate the rock strata in the pit.

An EVOLUTIONIST said:

"You are a rejected mutant destined to be removed from the evolutionary cycle." In other words, he is going to DIE in the pit, so that he cannot produce any "pit-falling offspring."

An I.R.S. man asked if he was paying taxes on the pit.

The COUNTY INSPECTOR asked if he had a permit to dig a pit.

A PROFESSOR gave him a lecture on: *The Elementary Principles of the Pit.*

An EVASIVE person avoided the subject of his pit altogether.

A SELF-PITYING person said:

"You haven't seen anything until you've seen MY PIT!!"

JIMMY THE GREEK said:

"CHANCES are that anyone could fall into a pit."

A VALLEY GIRL said:

"It's really you, Sweets. IT's your decor!!"

A CHARISMATIC said:

"Just CONFESS that you're not in a pit."

An OPTIMIST said:

"Things COULD be worse."

A PESSIMIST said:

"Things WILL get worse!!"

JESUS, seeing the man, took him by the hand and LIFTED HIM OUT of the pit.

"1988 is the year we bring the entire planet to Christ. 1989 is the year we party."

From Issue #97/June-July, 1987

From Issue #88/December, 1985–January, 1986

ONE EUNUCH IS ENOUGH

A Revisionist Reading of Acts 8:26-40

Philip, having nothing better to do, went south from Jerusalem to Gaza along the desert road. And behold, an Ethiopian eunuch, a representative in the parley of the United Front for Ethiopians, had come to Jerusalem to worship and was returning. Seated in his chauffeured Mercedes, the eunuch was reading the prophet Isaiah. Philip waved as the car went by, so the eunuch had the driver turn around and catch Philip at the next rest stop.

"I want you to explain this reading to me," said the eunuch.

"Oh, I couldn't do that," said Philip. "I wouldn't want to violate the integrity of your native faith by introducing Judeo-Christian Western concepts."

"But I want to hear the good news about Jesus Christ whom God has raised from the dead," said the eunuch.

"Well, I'm glad you appreciate the mythical power of our preaching, but I see no need for you to denigrate centuries of native African oral tradition in favor of our pre-Enlightenment, non-historical/scientific apparition accounts."

"But you don't understand -- I want to repent of my sins and receive the forgiveness of God. I want to live the new life of the risen Lord. See, here is water. What prevents me from being baptized?"

"Well, of course, religion is a private thing, and whatever you want to do is fine with me. After all, I wouldn't want to get pushy . . . Maybe you should go to church or something."

With that, the eunuch drove off in disgust, but Philip found himself in Azotus, took an aerobics class, and visited a local seminary where he was asked to teach a class on wine tasting.

—William H. Shepherd, Jr.

From Issue #35/February-March, 1977

From Issue #57/October-November, 1980

Being Cool

By Mike Yaconelli

From Issue #90/April-May, 1986

It has happened to me again. A friend of mine became a Christian. I have known him for many years and have always been concerned about his relationship with God. In the past couple of years, he made some very bad decisions about his life, and I wondered if he would ever be open to the Gospel. But I didn't want to rush into talking to him about Jesus. I wanted to take it slow—to win his confidence. I didn't want to take any chances of offending him.

While I was waiting for the right moment, someone he worked with came up to him one day and asked, "Are you going to heaven or hell?" Can you believe that? How tacky. How insensi-

tive and un-cool. It must have been a tract-wielding fundamentalist. But . . . uh . . . my friend had never been asked that question. It bothered him. He decided he didn't want to go to a place called "hell." To make a long story short, my friend continued talking to the "fanatic" and became a Christian. Now he is preparing to go to Bible school so he can be a minister.

Uh . . . you don't suppose this strategy of trying not to offend people is flawed, do you? You don't suppose that the Gospel *is* offensive by definition? You don't suppose that anytime you talk to people about Jesus, you risk offending them? Or that being offended just might be part of the process of conversion?

It doesn't matter. Offending people runs against my grain. As a matter of fact, it's been a long time since I have offended anyone. Of course, I do manage to offend someone in every issue of *The Door*, but that is not the kind of offending I am talking about. I am talking about offending someone because of the Gospel. I am talking about making someone uncomfortable because I am asking them to respond to the claim of Jesus Christ on their life. Nope. Not me. I'm too sophisticated now. Too cool. I don't believe in that kind of offensiveness anymore. I believe in "winning the right to be heard" and "relational evangelism" and "witnessing by doing rather than by saying." Very respectable. And, I must say, very effective. I can't think of any of my friends who have been offended by my faith in Christ.

I just finished reading *The Myth of Certainty*, a brilliant book by Daniel Taylor. Mr. Taylor describes a fictional teacher at a typically conservative, evangelical Bible College. Sarah, the teacher, is asked why she has put up with such a theologically narrow and intellectually rigid institution for over fifty years of teaching.

She replies:

" . . . I don't know if you can understand this, (but) it would have been giving up those people who care about me the most. They are the people who cared enough to patiently teach me all the antiquated traditions, all the sentimental songs, all their silly, little idiosyncrasies, so that I, Sarah Lawrence, could be one of God's people. And, you know, in the midst of all that hodgepodge of fundamentalist faith, and populist politics, and work ethic capitalism, and farmer's almanac science, and midwestern dullness, and other odd pieces of string, I somehow met God. Amongst these people, He first called me by name, and said, 'Sarah, I will be your God, and you will be one of my people.' How do you walk away from that . . . ?"

How do you walk away from that? I don't think you can. And that is why I have some difficulty with Fundamentalists Anonymous. I can understand not being a fundamentalist anymore, but I can't understand not being grateful to my fundamentalist heritage for helping me meet God. That's it, isn't it? That *is* what matters—people meeting God.

Sarah Lawrence was able to put up with all of the absurdities of the fundamentalists around her because, in the midst of those absurdities, they helped her find God. I guess that is why I still hang around the conservative church. In spite of all the inconsistency, in spite of all the narrow-mindedness and legalistic nonsense, evangelicals and fundamentalists are still committed to helping people meet God.

There is a lot I don't like about fundamentalists, but when it comes to a passion to help people meet God, no one comes close to them. I am cool and sophisticated, but I can't help but wonder, "How many people have met God through their association with cool and sophisticated Mike in the past year?"

Reports From The Mission Field

By Jerry Kelty and Dan Rupple

From Issue #95/February-March, 1987

Dear Pastor Benosic and the Beloved Congregation at-large:

On behalf of my brother Otto and myself, I want to sincerely thank you for your continued support and your earnest prayers. We so appreciate the many wonderful gifts you have sent over the past few months. We'd especially like to thank Jed and Delores Cook for the wonderful Hi-Tech Toaster Oven. It has been a source of amazement to the tribesmen, as well as providing hours of laughter among the village children. If we ever get electricity, we may consider plugging it in.

We'd also like to thank the Morgans for the shipment of clothes. We understand with your daughters all grown, a surplus was created and we appreciate you keeping us in mind. The sweaters and jeans were especially welcomed, but unfortunately we didn't have much use for the five prom dresses. The native women, although, did enjoy the homecoming tiaras. They've become quite the status symbol.

You may recall that we mentioned our need for aluminum foil. After a big hunt we'll wrap an entire boar (and I don't mean Otto, ha) in foil for cooking. Well, imagine our surprise when Mrs. Ferguson's fourth grade class sent us 25 pounds of foil...all in gum wrappers. Little, bitty gum wrappers. It took us four days to dice the meat. Thank God Ben Jacobs had sent us that Veg-a-matic.

We have learned an awful lot about relating to another culture this year. We originally approached the tribe with 500 Four Spiritual Law tracts. They were well received. Rolled up, they make perfect studs after a nose-piercing session. Since then, we have tried to meet them a little more on their level. Which reminds me, the Christian rap records were wonderful, but

Chief Zoobe wants to know if you have any James Brown. Maybe his "good God" yelp will open a door of utterance.

Hope to hear from you soon and may God bless you for your intentions.

D ear Friends:
Greetings. A lot has happened since I last wrote.

Just last week, I went down to the river bank and saw our unselfish dog, who we nicknamed Ol' Yeller, nursing a swarm of piranhas. At least that's what he thought he was doing. The piranhas thought they were at the 4.99 Smorgasdog.

There've also been quite a number of skeeters around lately—so many that my son Emmett, to whom God gave the gift of poetry, decided to write a poem about them. Here it is:

The air is heavy with hemoglobin
The mosquitoes are eating
The mosquitoes are eating
There's a little hole in the roof
The mosquitoes find it
The mosquitoes aren't dumb
Don't go outside right now
They're practicing their dive-bomb-
*   ing missions*
On you
Don't forget
They don't have anything else to do

Pray for a new boat for the wife and me, this one's half sinking. Oh, and a new dog. 🔑

MATTHEW 25
CONTEMPORIZED

By Marv Hinten

From Issue #91/June-July, 1986

After several months of working in a Christian bookstore, I know what types of books our customers buy most often. And it sometimes seems that Jesus' teaching about the judgment should be rewritten thusly:

Then will He say to those at His left, "I was hungry, and you bought another Christian diet plan; thirsty, and you bought books on the end times; I was a stranger, and you read religious romances; naked, and you pored over your personal color analysis; ill and in prison and you studied how to achieve health and prosperity."

Then they will answer, "Lord, when did we see you hungry or thirsty or a stranger or naked or ill or in prison and did not serve you?"

Then He will answer them, "I assure you, insofar as you failed to read books on service and maturity, and read only books on Christian self-gratification, you failed to know my needs."

From Issue #95/February-March, 1987

To Keep or Not to Keep the Audi

By Bob Lupton

From Issue #105/May-June, 1989

At Christmastime, a friend presented us with the keys to a shiny black 1983 Audi 5000 Turbo Diesel! We were speechless. It was a beautiful automobile—one owner, well-maintained, and an ideal size for our family. Such a fine gift was beyond our most aggressive dreaming and praying.

We slipped into the leather seats, adjusted them to fit our posture, and pulled out of the drive for our first check-out ride. It was sheer delight to feel a fine automobile respond to the touch. A superb stereo system wrapped us in classical sounds. It may have been a function of our own enthrallment, but it seemed that people took more notice of us than when we were in the Datsun. Americans and Luptons love quality. What a wonderful gift from God.

A couple of days after receiving the car, I was giving a journalist a tour of our ministry to the poor. As I drove him past our home, he spied the Audi sitting in the driveway. I wished immediately that it were parked out of sight behind the house. I wondered what assumptions were silently forming in the writer's mind, what questions the car had raised about my integrity or that of the ministry. I wanted to explain to him how the car was an answer to prayer, not a symbol of self-indulgence. I wanted him to know that it was not as new as it looked, that it was a gift. To explain, of course, would only make me appear defensive, so I said nothing. I hoped he would conclude that the car belonged to someone else.

It was a gift from God, wasn't it—an answer to our prayers? Why then do we feel this uneasiness about others seeing the car? For years, I have been bothered by the TV evangelists who own gold Mercedes and Lear jets, and the lady preacher of a poor church in our community who drives a new pink Cadillac Eldorado convertible that she says God gave her. To get rich from ministry, to lounge in self-indulgent comfort at the expense of the poor, is just plain sin. I am appalled by the gross perversion of truth that Jim and Tammy Faye Bakker have exemplified.

But the Audi is different. It's not a Mercedes or a Cadillac. It's much further down on the list of prestige automobiles. It reflects good stewardship—excellent gas mileage, no car payment, a long-life diesel engine. And it is worth much more to drive than to trade. Trading down to a Chevy or Toyota would necessitate an auto loan, and debt is something we are trying to avoid.

LIFESTYLE EVANGELISM

ED'S TOWING AND WORSHIP

HALL

From Double Issue #98–99/ AugustSeptember–October–November,

Good stewardship leads us to keep the Audi and enjoy it as a blessing from God.

At a dinner table discussion the other night, Jeff, our seventeen-year-old, commented that it seemed rather dishonest to him for us to even consider trading the Audi just to play into a "humble missionary" image. Certainly we are rich by the standard of most of our neighbors. For all of our urban lifestyle adjustments, we are still rich. An Audi is an authentic expression of that reality. Peggy added that it didn't seem fair that our decisions should be controlled by the perceptions and expectations of others who watch from a distance. We know that the Audi makes perfect sense for us. Why should we let concern over the uninformed judgments of others rob us of our joy? The Audi is honest and it is right.

How strange it is that over the last few days I have heard the voice of my Dad replaying from the memories of my childhood. Though he has been gone for some years now, his words return with remarkable clarity. "Avoid the very appearance of evil." His quote from Scripture speaks of values of a different sort. The words call for a sensitivity to the lifestyle struggles of others. They are words that caution against wounding the conscience of a fragile believer or of causing young faith to turn cynical. They are words about Audis—the honest and right things in life—that must be relinquished for the sake of others. The Audi is good. But to use money given for ministry among the poor to support instead the luxurious lifestyle of an urban worker—that is evil. Even the appearance of such is to be shunned.

So what is the higher value—good stewardship or avoiding the appearance of evil? And what about the hypocrisy of driving a "humble" car when we can really afford better? Our motives are never pure anyway. Christians aren't supposed to judge each other, so why become captive to their uninformed opinions?

I would like to continue this irrational filibuster for the next several years while I enjoy driving the Audi. But when I become still before God, I am aware of that gentle nudging, familiar to all believers, toward the laying down of life and other valued things for the sake of sisters and brothers.

Thank you, dear friend, for your generous and thoughtful gift. Though we cannot keep the Audi, it has brought us joy, struggle, and a deeper understanding of the life in Christ to which we have all been called.

THE HEALING OF MY THEOLOGY

By Tony Campolo

From Issue #57/October-November, 1980

A few years back I was involved in a charismatic experience. It was very impressive. I was speaking at a small Midwest university (a semi-religious Methodist college) for their Religious Emphasis Week. On Wednesday night of that week, a woman came walking down the aisle carrying a little boy with leg braces. I was in the middle of my talk, so I stopped talking and asked if I could help her. She said, "God told me to come. He told me that you would heal my child." I was speechless. I tried to regain my composure and explained to the woman that there were a variety of gifts: the gift of preaching, the gift of teaching, the gift of healing, and many others. I told her I did not have the gift of healing. (I felt like saying, "If I could heal,

would I look like this?") But she just kept standing there. She looked directly into my eyes and said, "But God told me."

At this point, the college chaplain (a Princeton model complete with turtle neck, medallion, and pipe) asked if he could help. I was hoping he would politely usher her out of the meeting. Instead, he asked everyone at the meeting, "How many of you absolutely believe this child is going to be healed tonight?" Four students raised their hands . . . they were Pentecostal. Then the chaplain did a remarkable thing. He asked everyone who didn't believe that the little boy could be healed to leave the room. He pointed out that even Jesus could do no mighty works while surrounded by unbelief. (I thought to myself, "Not bad for a Princeton guy.") Actually, I began to think he was a very smooth operator. With everyone gone, it was beginning to look like I was off the hook. But I wasn't off the hook. The woman was still standing there.

The chaplain suggested that we all go into the back room and pray for the boy's healing and anoint his head with oil. Feeling increasingly uneasy, I asked him what kind of oil we would use. He answered, "Del Monte." I was feeling uncomfortable with all of this and expressed my feelings to the chaplain. He reminded me that when we don't know what to do, do what the Bible says. And in the book of James, it says, "Bring them to the elders, lay hands and anoint their heads with oil." (Again, not bad for a Princeton guy.)

We all went into the back room—the chaplain, the woman and her boy, the four Pentecostals, and myself. We formed a circle around the crippled boy, laid hands on him, and the chaplain anointed him with oil. It looked like half time at a basketball game. I started praying one of those perfunctory prayers you learn in seminary. I didn't know what else to do. I felt awkward, embarrassed, and out of my realm. The Pentecostal kids were doing their thing with the chanting and speaking in tongues. In the midst of all this pandemonium, I was asking myself what I was doing there. I just wanted to get out of there and . . . suddenly . . . the Holy Spirit came upon us. How did I know? All I can say is that when the Holy Spirit comes upon you, you know. An awe fell over all of us and the room went silent. We all sensed the presence of the Holy Spirit. It was overpowering. We withdrew our hands, and I fully expected the boy to be healed. He wasn't.

Three years later, I was speaking at the Third Baptist Church in St. Louis, and a woman came up to me after the meeting. She asked if I remembered her. I couldn't place her. Smiling, she told me that she was the woman who had come to me three years before with a little boy who needed healing. I remembered, of course, and reluctantly asked how her little boy was doing. She turned and said, "There he is." He came running towards me with legs as straight and whole as they could be. I was stunned.

"What happened?" I asked.

She smiled. "We prayed . . . remember?"

But nothing had happened, I thought. She went on to explain that the next morning after our prayer, her son had awakened crying. He complained that his braces were too tight, so they were loosened a little, and his legs seemed a little bit straighter. This went on every morning for the next month until his legs were perfectly straight. He had been healed.

I must be honest. I have always been skeptical of that kind of thing. My non-healing bias and my "enlightened" theology did not allow for healing. But there, in the beauty of that moment, I realized that God is greater than my theology. I learned that God is able to do abundantly above what any of us could ever think or hope for. Not only had a little boy been healed, but so had my theology.

3

The Membrane That Connects Your Tongue to the Bottom of Your Mouth

Communication

Sometimes strange or seemingly insignificant things can drastically affect our ability to communicate. For example, that odd-looking little membrane that connects our tongue to the bottom of our mouth. If we didn't have it, we wouldn't be able to talk. In fact, we would only be able to grunt and snarl at each other, which is not how human beings communicate— well, except at Southern Baptist conventions. That one little membrane holds the key to much of our communication.

And as you know, *The Door* has always been committed to crisp, clear communication. For instance, when an interview with Harvey Cox in 1976 became hopelessly jumbled during layout, the Doorkeepers decided they couldn't stand idly by and watch the communication process fall apart. Two issues later they made the following valiant effort to direct readers through the maze of that interview. (Believe it or not, these directions actually work.)

"Step 1. From the bottom of page 6, move directly to the *far right column of page 7*. Read down 7 3/8 inches of print through the sentence that ends with 'in everyday.'

"Step 2. Move directly across the page *to the left-hand column of page 7*. Continue reading with *The Door* question that asks, 'Could you illustrate?' Read to the bottom of this column.

"Step 3. Immediately move *to the top of the left-hand column of page 7*. Read all the way down the column to the point where *The Door* asks the question, 'Could you illustrate?' (You've already been there once, remember?)

"Step 4. Move directly across the page *to the right-hand column of page 7* and begin reading with 'sexuality is taken very seriously by the' and finish the page.

"Step 5. Continue reading the interview as if nothing out of the ordinary had occurred."

Now that's communication at its finest.

The Door has also shown amazing versatility in its analysis of communication, exploring all types of creative expression—television, newspapers, drama, poetry, advertising, radio, books, and music.

For example, in 1979 *The Door* introduced H. Winfield Tutte's new smash album,

Pews. This work of art prompted the *Reader's Digest* to note, "The unique combination of these minds keeps us from going outside at night." *Pews* failed to go platinum (for sales of a million or more copies), but it did manage to go polyester (for sales of 7 or 8).

Then in 1986 Joel Rasmussen took *Door* readers into the exciting world of romance novel publishing when he made a plug for such classic Christian romances as *Biological Ecstasy*, the story of Tom and Liz, who fall desperately in love during biology class.

As Rasmussen put it, "Conflict erupts when Tom discovers that Liz is a theistic evolutionist, while he is a committed creationist. Their relationship deteriorates when a drive-in date turns into a discussion of the second law of thermodynamics versus Cambrian vertebrates in a closed ecosystem. Liz softens a bit after reading *From Goo to You, By Way of the Zoo*, but a stormy future still lies ahead. Will Tom concede the existence of Piltdown man? Will Liz be able to produce examples of transitional forms?"

I don't have the answer to those questions. But if you want to peek at *The Door*'s contributions in numerous areas of communication— news writing, magazine and book publishing, television, music, art, computerized mailings, and typographical errors—just keep reading. 🔑

From Issue #69/
October–November, 1982

NEWS BRIEFS

Doug Peterson

The United States has long maintained three vehicles of nuclear attack—one by land, one by air and one by sea. Today, the Pentagon announced plans to construct a fourth vehicle of attack; a system that is the most deadly of them all.

"We plan to use old church buses to carry multiple individually targeted reentry missiles," said General John Brack. According to Brack, each bus will carry some of the most advanced equipment, all designed to fool Soviet radar and make the vehicle look like a normal bus on its way to a church camp near Moscow."

To be more specific, each bus will be designed to make 5,432 potty stops, 567,000 stops at McDonald's restaurants, suffer 314 flat tires and other varieties of mechanical failure, and make 765 wrong turns.

For added realism, a tape of someone yelling, "Shut up back there!" will play continuously.

The only difficulty so far has been finding chaperones. Many parents thought the mission was too dangerous; but once it was clarified that they would be travelling with a nuclear bomb, and not a bus-load of kids, there were more than enough volunteers.

(From Issue #68/August–September, 1982)

Rev. Gregory Jones, pastor of the First Christian Church in Hypothermia, Minnesota, is being held in connection with the death of church elder, Michael Edwards.

Edwards was found meetinged to death in the church's Fellowship Hall last weekend. While the motive has yet to be discovered, authorities believe Rev. Jones strangled Edwards with the 156 committee meetings that the deceased elder was required to attend every week.

Authorities caution, however, that the body hasn't yet been positively identified as Edwards. Evidently, the Edwards' family is not sure if it is him.

"Michael was always at church," said the potential widow, Frida Edwards. "I forgot what he looks like."

(From Issue #69/October–November, 1982)

Senator Sam Thurtle, from Massachusetts, was released from the Boston Politician's Hospital today after nearly choking to death on one of his campaign promises.

The incident began when Thurtle tried to muster the support of black religious leaders at a lunch yesterday. The religious leaders, suspicious of white insincerity, were not willing to swallow his extravagant promises and Thurtle became flustered.

In an attempt to prove that his promises were sincere and edible, Thurtle swallowed several of them himself, and he immediately began to choke.

"That crazy guy tried to swallow 14 promises whole!" exclaimed one religious leader, Rev. Tom Parker. "If there hadn't been a medic handy to give him a tracheotomy, he'd be politically dead right now."

The choking incident renewed the controversy over whether it is really possible for blacks to extract sincere promises from white politicians. Some believe it is possible to do so by using nonviolent actions, such as sit-ins and marches, though many support use of "the Malcolm X Maneuver." This first-aid technique, which is posted in restaurants wherever politicians gather, suggests that you get behind the politician, wrap your arms around him and thrust upwards into his ribs, forcing a sincere promise to pop out like a cork from a bottle.

(From Issue #77/February–March, 1984)

The Evangelical Gossip Columnist's Academy decided yesterday that the number-one scandal story of the year was the separation of church and state. Members of the American Civil Liberties Union were on hand to present the honor, while entertainment was provided by Warren Burger and the Supremes.

As the scandal presently stands, the church and state are legally separated, and they are just beginning divorce proceedings.

The messy conflict dates back to when the state first began to stay out late with the boys and then come home with evolution on its breath. However, problems didn't become intense until the state tried to keep the church out of politics by claiming that "a church's place is in the home."

Finally, the straw that broke every bone in the camel's body came when the state was seen around town with secular humanism on one arm and Carl Sagan on the other. Church and state are now grappling over custody of the children's minds.

"I think it's all a mistake," said a disturbing report from a disturbed reported. "The church and state originally didn't expect things to go this far. They only planned to have separate checking accounts."

(From Issue #76/December, 1983–January, 1984)

"When is a child able to accept Christ?" is just one of the questions posed by Holly Thompson's tantalizing new self-help book on parenthood, *You Call Yourself a Parent? Make Me Laugh.*

According to Thompson, she sides with Thomas Aquinas, who said that children can accept Christ when they reach "the Age of Reason." Unfortunately, the Age of Reason is only a ten-minute period. It starts around the child's seventh birthday and ends when you have to explain to him that stomping on sparks is a good way to put out a campfire but not a good idea for putting out his birthday candles.

Thompson says she is presently working on a sequel, tentatively entitled *Why Everything You Do as a Parent is Wrong.* In it, she coins catchy child-rearing phrases, such as, "You can lead a horse to water, but you can't make him drink," and the toilet-training classic, "You can lead a two-year-old to the bathroom, but you can't make him tinkle."

In this new book, Thompson says that a parent should create an atmosphere of trust. Dependability is important in this frightening world, so it is best that children be exposed only to Japanese products until, say, eight years of age.

"A child is a gift from God," Thompson adds. "Which explains why most parents look for a receipt and try to exchange this gift whenever they discover that their kid spent the afternoon exploding potatoes in the microwave."

(From Double Issue #98–99/August–September–October–November, 1987)

The Internal Revenue Service, which jailed cult leader Sun Myung Moon several years ago for tax evasion, has decided there's something to learn from cults. "The IRS decided the most effective way to collect taxes was to use the fund-raising techniques of cults," said one IRS representative just prior to chanting,

"Hare taxes, hare taxes. Taxes,

taxes. Hare, hare."

IRS agents, now part of a full-fledged cult known as the "Monies," can be routinely seen in airports, soliciting money, selling flowers, conducting love audits, and telling people the world will end every April 15.

The Monies also have learned a few tips from Christian organizations. For example, they developed their own plan of salvation based on Campus Crusade for Christ's "Four Spiritual Laws." In true form, the IRS has complicated the plan of salvation with its "15,678 Spiritual Laws in Very Fine Print."

According to the plan, "You can reach salvation if you subtract the number of sins on line 22a of Schedule F from the amount of earned grace on line 4t of Schedule L, then add the number of karma credits and impersonal deductions from lines..."

(From Issue #101/February–March, 1988)

MARGIN NOTES

Classical music is played as background to professional boxing matches in Thailand.

Seventy-two muscles are used in speaking one word.

The accordion was invented in 1829, by Damian of Vienna.

People like to sing in the bathtub because they can hear themselves easily in a small, highly reverberant room.

St. Patrick was not an Irishman. He was born in Britain.

Amy Grant: "I Was Raised By Family of Wild Wolfhounds"

The DOOR has learned that at the age of 7 months, while on a family outing at Trout Haven, off of highway 385 near Lead, South Dakota, Amy was carried away by a pack of timber wolves.

For the next 11 years she was nurtured, protected and taught survival instincts by the animals of the wild.

AMY today.   **WALLET PHOTO** she still keeps.

During the day she would roam the Black Hills' forests with other beasts of prey in search of her meals. At night, she would join with the predators to howl at the moon. "I look back at my childhood experiences and laugh," Amy ad-

mitted, "I had no idea how the Lord would one day work through these things to give me the kind of perspective anyone in today's, shall I say, 'Dog Eat Dog' world of contemporary Christian

(continued on page 37)[1]

Dear Abbot

Concerning Mints and Make-up

DEAR ABBOT: Last week, my husband and I had a lovely dinner with a couple I'll call Mary and Steve. We were taken aback, however, when Mary served the after-dinner mints *before* dessert. Since Mary and I are good friends, I hinted later that it was proper etiquette to bring out the mints after the *entire* dinner, dessert included. But she said if that were true, then the candies would be called "after-dessert mints." Abbot, who is right? —MINT CONDITION INQUIRER

DEAR MINT CONDITION: I think you're avoiding the real issue here, and that is your relationship with Jesus Christ. You know, the Bible tells us that Jesus is the way, the truth and the life. He is the answer to all our questions, the solution to all our problems.

DEAR ABBOT: Several years ago, you responded to a letter from a mother whose 12-year-old daughter had demanded the right to get her ears pierced, dye her hair, wear make-up and start smoking. I am now facing a similar problem with my son. Could you please find and reprint the answer to that letter? — MOROSE MOTHER

DEAR MOROSE MOM: It took me awhile to track it down, but here is the reply you asked about:

I think you're avoiding the real issue here, and that is

your relationship with Jesus Christ. You know, the Bible tells us that Jesus is the way, the truth and the life. He is the answer to all our questions, the solution to all our problems.

CONFIDENTIAL TO BATTERED WIFE IN TEXAS: I think you're avoiding the real issue here, and that is your relationship with Jesus Christ. You know, the Bible tells us that Jesus is the way, the truth and the life. He is the answer to all our questions, the solution to all our problems.

By Roy Rivenburg
From Issue #76/December, 1983–January, 1984

---

[1] By Kraig Klaudt. From Issue #69/October–November, 1982. There was no page 37 in that issue.

ABOVE: From Issue #45/
October–November, 1976
LEFT: From Issue #76/
December, 1983–January, 1984
BELOW: From Issue #76/
December, 1983–January, 1984

Also in the News

NATION
Solution to nativity scene controversy proposed: invisible creche figures perceptible only through special glasses available at Christian bookstores. B-3.

BOOKS
"How-to" books condemned as unbiblical; "How-not-to" series in the works. D-11.

PEWS
National Council recommends "Finders/Keepers" policy regarding loose change found between the cracks in church seating. C-14.

DRIVE-IN FUNERAL HOMES: AN AFFAIR TO REMEMBER

CHICAGO—A Chicago funeral home has set up a drive-through service, complete with cameras and a sound system, which allows busy visitors to pay their last respects, sign the funeral register, and view the remains of a friend or loved one—all without ever leaving the comfort of their own automobile.

The New York Times News Service reports that Gatling's Funeral Home on Chicago's South Side instituted the service more than two years ago. A complex system of switches and relays allows as many as a dozen bodies to be viewed.

Owner Lafayette Gatling originally came up with the idea because he used to feel uncomfortable coming to a funeral home in soiled clothes. But he says the system has been particularly helpful when the deceased was having an affair and both a wife and a girlfriend wanted to pay their respects.

"This way, the girlfriend can go through the drive-through and pay her respects in whatever name she chooses, while the wife is inside with the deceased," Gatling says. "It happens all the time."

From Issue #108/ November-December, 1989

ELVIS VIRUS

A chilling statistic from *The Dallas Morning News*: According to a recent study, when Elvis Presley was alive, there were 34 Elvis impersonators. Presently, there are 8,029. The report calculated that, at the current rate, one out of every five people on earth will be an Elvis impersonator by the year 2037.

From Issue #104/March–April, 1989

SUED FOR BEING OVERWEIGHT?

A police officer who hurt his back while lifting a 300-pound abortion protestor has filed suit against the protestor and his sponsoring group. The officer has asked for unspecified punitive and compensatory damages against a Waco man for being so overweight during a religious protest at an Austin abortion clinic.

From Issue #109/ January–February, 1990

WHEN THE ROLL IS CALLED WILL YOU BE THERE?

Will you be one of the 5,473,000,000 elect, give or take a few Mormons? *LandMARC*, a magazine published by "MARC Europe," arrived at 5,473,000,000 as the current population of Heaven by first adding up all of the deaths since 40,000 B.C.— which works out to be about 60 billion stiffs through 1980. The publication then took the estimates from 8,000 B.C. onward and figured out the world's Christian population since that time. (The figures for that dicey bit of information were provided by David Barrett's *World Christian Encyclopedia*.)

From Issue #105/May–June, 1989

NUKE AND NUN NONSENSE

CINCINNATI—The Association to Save Madonna From Nuclear War (we SWEAR we're not making this up), an Ohio-based philosophical/anti-nuclear war organization, wants the government to declare a "nuclear-free zone" within a 200-mile radius of anyplace Madonna is.

We kid you not.

From Issue #107/ September–October, 1989

TOP: From Issue #48/
April–May, 1979;
RIGHT: From Issue #96/
April–May, 1987;
BELOW: From Issue #69/
October–November, 1982

TV GUIDE POST

Wednesday

7:30 🔢 **$700 CLUB—Talk**

8:30 🔟 **KUKLA, FRAN AND TIM LaHAYE**
The four temperaments of the male are portrayed with hand puppets.

9 AM 🔟 **$20,000 CATHEDRAL—Game**
Robert Schuller, host.
🔢 **YOU BET YOUR ABUNDANT LIFE—Game**

10 AM 🔢 **AGAPE BOAT**
🔢 **I AGAPE LUCY**
🔢 **AGAPE, AMERICAN STYLE**
🔢 **THE LOST IN SPACE - Ex-traterrestrial Evangelism**

11:30 🔢 **AS THE WORLD COUNCIL OF CHURCHES TURNS—Serial**
The political career of the Catholics is tarnished when their affair with the Charismatics is revealed. The Lutherans, after a bitter separation, make another go at it.

12 PM 🔢 **SHA NA NA—Glossolalia**

12:30 🔢 **LEAVE IT TO BELIEVER—Comedy**

1 PM 🔟 **FATHER KNOWS (In the Biblical Sense) BEST**
A sultry TV drama based on Andrew Greeley novels.
🔢 **WIDE WORLD OF SPIRITS—Adventure**
Demons are exorcised in Acapulco and spells are broken in Europe. Kenneth E. Hagin, host.
🔢 **GENTILE BEN—Anti-Semitic Animal Adventure**

2 PM 🔢 **THE WILD, WILD WESTMINSTER SEMINARY**
John Murray (Robert Conrad) and Charles Hodge (Ross Martin) expose various radical theological groups at Princeton.
🔢 **ALL IN THE FAMINE—Situation Comedy**
Carroll O'Connor stars as a ghetto-dwelling welfare recipient whose conservative son-in-law wants to become an Amway salesman.

2:30 🔢 **MOVIE—Drama**
"Falwell to Arms" (1979) Hemingway's famous posthumous account of the Moral Majority and national defense.

3 PM 🔟 **LITTLE RADICALS—Comedy**
Alf Alfa (Ronald Sider) and Buckwheat (John Perkins) T.P. a nuclear power plant.

3:30 🔢 **THE BROTHER LAWRENCE WELK SHOW—Contemplative Waltz**

5:30 🔢 **WILD KINGDOM COME—Eschatology**
🔢 **THE WONDERFUL WORLD OF LINDSEY**
Feature. "Herbie the Posche Targa" (1977).

6 PM 🔟 **THE HONEYMOONIES**
Ralph and Norton stage a mass wedding.

7 PM 🔢 **B.J. AND THE BEAR—Adventure**
A famous Christian vocalist and a former Alabama football coach team up to drive a Sunday school bus.

7:30 🔢 **DIFF'RENT STROKES—Pentecostal Suspense**
This week, believers are healed of thrombosis.
🔢 **THREE'S TRINITY—Comedy**
In this episode a Jehovah's Witness, a Unitarian and a Wheaton Bible prof. are trapped alone in the same room.

8 PM 🔟 **REAL PAPAL—Human Interest**
Pope John Paul talks about custom van designing.
🔢 **FANTASY ISLAND**
Tattoo welcomes people to an unreal island where TV evangelists open their financial records to the public and don't wear hairspray.
🔢 **ANGLEY'S ANGELS**
The eccentric millionaire Ernest Angley employs three shapely celestial spirits to watch over his ministry.

9 PM 🔢 **DALLAS—Drama**
Things get pretty serious for the seminary gang as they translate a Bible together and inadvertently leave out Mt. 5 and I Cor. 12-14.
🔟 **MAGNUM, P.K.**
Rugged Vacation Bible School adventures with a macho minister's son.

10 PM 🔢 🔟 🔢 **NEWS**

10:30 🔢 **LATE NIGHT MOVIE**
"King Kung" (1970). The primate cannot be subdued as he swings carefree from the dome of St. Peter's.
🔟 **THE SAINT—Crime Drama**
Simon goes undercover as a carnal Christian to smuggle Gideon Bibles into the Moscow Hilton. Simon: Bro. Andrew.

—Kraig Klaudt

By Dan Pegoda
From Issue #81/
October–November, 1984

ART AND SATIRE

The Door
Mini-Interview

Dan Pegoda

From Issue #90/
April–May, 1986

Dan Pegoda, former art director for The Door *is a quiet man. So quiet that it was three years after he started working for* The Door *before we knew he was working for us.*

Dan Pegoda. Shy. Unassuming. He doesn't talk, he whispers—which is really annoying because when you are talking to someone who whispers, it makes you whisper. Now everyone in our office is whispering.

When we suggested to Dan the idea of doing a Door *interview, he refused and wouldn't speak to us for three weeks (which we didn't realize for six weeks because he normally doesn't speak to us for three weeks). When we explained to him that an interview would be a growth experience for him and would also keep him from being fired, he graciously accepted.*

Dan Pegoda is a man of few words, but when you see what those words are . . . well . . .

Door: Well, Dan, how does it feel to be interviewed by your own magazine?
Dan: Fine.
Door: There is no doubt that over the years, as your artistic talents have been honed and refined, *The Door* has reflected that honement and refinement.
Dan: Honement?
Door: Yes. The process whereby art does more than reflect or imitate reality but, instead, actually becomes reality. It is the process whereby the person doing the art, as a person, becomes an artist who reflects art in their personness—where art becomes more than art; it becomes a part of, an expression of, the person doing the art, the artist himself. Isn't that exactly what is happening in *The Door*? You, Dan—the artist, the art director, the artiste, the persona of art—you create, through your art, a magazine that is more than a magazine. It is . . . well . . . it is you!
Dan: Uh . . .
Door: *The Door* is a satirical magazine. Obviously, a satirical magazine demands something different from an artist.
Dan: . . .
Door: The point is that satire as satire is one thing, whereas satire and art—
Dan: —are two things.
Door: And when these two things are brought together, then art becomes satirical art, which is—
Dan: —one thing again.
Door: It is very clear to us, Dan, that art as structure, as line and form, form and line, and as defined in *The Door* has matured as *The Door* has matured.
Dan: Uh . . . yeah, I guess so.
Door: Time marches on. Things change. You change. The Church changes. The world changes. Inevitably, *The Door* changes. The question on all of our minds is, where do you go from here?
Dan: I'm going over to my folks' for dinner. 🔑

ABOVE: From Issue #54/April–May, 1980
BELOW: From Issue #69/October–November, 1982

"I'd like to share a song with you that the
Lord gave me a year ago . . . and even
though he did give it to me, any
reproduction of this song in any form
without my written consent will constitute
infringement of copyright law which
grants me the right to sue your pants off
. . . praise God . . . "

Den
Hart

March 21, 1978

Chicken Take O. Cobbs
305 N. Beacon Boulevard
Grand Haven, Michigan 49417

Dear Chicken:

I am personally very grateful for your Faith Partner Commitment.

Because you and other friends answered my plea, Chicken, I now believe we will be able to keep The Old Time Gospel Hour on nearly all our present stations.

I know this is a joy to you personally, and I hope you will join me in prayer that we will now use this opportunity to bring others in your community -- and across the nation -- to a saving faith in Jesus Christ.

Each time you join me for a broadcast, I think you should take great pride in knowing it is YOUR Faith Partner commitment which is helping to make the program possible.

As I promised, Chicken, each month I'm going to write you a letter such as this discussing the controversial issues of our time --

-- and this month I want to talk to you about homosexuality -- one of the most serious sicknesses plaguing our society today.

Just 25 years ago the mere mention of the word "homosexual" was so revolting that most people wouldn't dare say it above a whisper.

Back then the act of homosexuality served as the height of contempt for God's Law -- and represented the lowest form of human behavior.

But not today!

From Issue #44/
August–September, 1978

THE OLD TIME GOSPEL HOUR   P.O. Box 1111   Lynchburg, VA 24505

4

Arms That Have No Feeling When You Wake Up Because You Slept on Them Wrong

Church Life

Occasionally I wake up and discover I have slept on one of my arms wrong and it has gone completely numb. But only once did I wake up to find *both* of my arms totally and completely asleep. What's more, the alarm clock was blaring away at a level that could wake people in Bolivia, so I had to swing my numb arms like floppy rope, hoping that one of them would hit the shut-off lever. After about a minute of thrashing around, I managed to knock the clock clear across the room, where it promptly stopped clanging.

Some churches are a lot like numb arms. Sound asleep.

Some have even been known to sleep through four Great Awakenings, although they may have gotten up once to go to the bathroom. Problems all around are screaming out for a response, yet some congregations sleep right through the alarm. Millions of people still need to hear the Gospel or fill their stomachs with a decent meal, while some churches spend months debating whether Moses got a farmer's tan wandering in the desert.

Keeping a congregation awake and on its toes requires hard work on the part of a lot of people, including senior pastors, assistant ministers, deacons, elders, lay persons, ushers, youth ministers, and a special new office that I like to call women-who-do-all-of-the-tasks-of-leadership-but-aren't-called-pastors-because-that-would-cause-half-of-the-membership-to-have-a-coronary.

This chapter is dedicated to all those hard-working individuals who constantly splash water in the congregation's face to keep it awake. It explores the inner workings of that wonderful creation called the church, with all of its idiosyncrasies, its programs, its organization, and its people.

When the New Jerusalem comes down from heaven at the end of time, maybe we won't need the church in its present form, with its committees and organizations and programs and such. But until then, we need it desperately. As Frederick Buechner points out in his book, *Wishful Thinking,* we need the church as much as Noah needed an ark.

" . . . and now I understand our organist has a little surprise for us this morning . . . "

Den Hart

From Issue #48/April–May, 1979

From Issue #17/February–March, 1974

PERFORMANCE APPRAISAL FOR CHURCH YOUTH WORKERS—Short Form
By Kathryn Lindskoog

PERFORMANCE FACTORS	FAR EXCEEDS JOB REQUIREMENTS	EXCEEDS JOB REQUIREMENTS	MEETS JOB REQUIREMENTS	NEEDS SOME IMPROVEMENT	DOES NOT MEET MINIMUM JOB REQUIREMENTS
VITALITY	Leaps tall buildings with a single bound.	Must take a running start to leap over tall buildings, especially those with spires.	Can run up two flights of stairs; knows how to use self-service elevator skillfully.	Often crashes into buildings in vain attempt to jump over them.	Can usually walk up one flight of stairs without gasping; some fear of escalators.
EFFICIENCY	Faster than a speeding bullet	As fast as a speeding bullet.	Not quite as fast as a speeding bullet.	Fast as a slowly rolling bullet.	Slower than a slowly rolling bullet.
ADAPT-ABILITY	Walks on water consistently.	Walks on water in emergencies.	Washes with water daily.	Washes with water occasionally.	Knees turn to water in emergencies.
INNER LIGHT	Sees God.	Hears God.	Talks to God.	Talks to self.	Won't listen to self.
INTELLECT	Has read all of Kittell and Ellul for fun (in the original German and French).	Has read all of the Anchor Bible and Schaeffer for fun.	Reads *The Door* for fun.	Can't read.	Can read but doesn't.
THEOLOGY	D.D., Th.D., Lit.D., Ph.D. Can recite entire Bible and Calvin's Commentaries. Has recently solved the problem of evil.	Has personally experienced every mode of spiritual blessing ever known in the history of the Christian Church.	Knows the Four Spiritual Laws; owns the Living Bible.	Knows "Bridge Over Troubled Water"; has seen "Ben Hur" and "The Ten Commandments."	Toying with possibility of joining Scientology next year.

A NEW PROPOSAL FOR THE CHURCH YEAR

Sunday Services Should Take On Important Issues— Study Reveals

By LeRoy Koopman

From Issue #69/
October–November, 1982

PROGRAM for Mercedes Benz Sunday.

Observing all the designated Sundays of the year can really be a hassle.

First, there's the church year. As the fundamentalists have dispensationalized the ages, so the liturgists have dispensationalized the year. The preacher feels obligated to observe Advent, Christmas, Epiphany, Lent, Easter, and Pentecost— each with its appropriate colors, ceremonies, Scripture readings, and vestments.

Then there is the civil year. Consider the challenge of squeezing into the preaching schedule appropriate references to Girl Scout Sunday, Boy Scout Sunday, Valentine's Day, St. Patrick's Day, Father's Day, Mother's Day, Children's Day, Grandparent's Day, Memorial Day, Independence Day, Labor Day, Columbus Day, and Thanksgiving—to say nothing of Law and Order Month, Get Out to Vote Week, Orchid Day, Pork Month, and National Pickle Week.

Thirdly, there are the missives from denominational offices urging observance of the denominational year (of-

fering to "resource" such events with an "intergenerational and cross-cultural experience kit"). A true and loyal minister, says the official literature, promotes Stewardship Sunday, Christian College Sunday, World Hunger Sunday, Universal Bible Sunday, Missions Emphasis Month, and Pensions Sunday, to name just a few.

All of these Sundays tend to gang up on the poor preacher. What does he do, for instance, when Ascension Sunday, which is also the Seventh Sunday after Easter, falls on Memorial Day Sunday, Graduation Sunday, and Support Your Missionaries in Kenya Sunday? Furthermore, what does he do when these Sundays imposed from the outside fail to reflect the true emphasis of his church?

Because of these difficulties, I'd like to suggest that the churches abandon the stereotypes of the church year, the civil year, and the denominational year, and concentrate instead on the issues *they* really believe are important. For a start, here are some suggestions for churches of various theological persuasions.

The Grace Bible Churches of the Separated Saints could observe Anti-WCC Sunday, Anti-NCC Sunday, Anti-Evolution Sunday, Anti-Homosexual Sunday, Anti-Rock Music Sunday, Anti-Gun Control Sunday, Anti-

Secular Humanism Sunday, Anti-Public Schools Sunday, Anti-Communism Sunday, Anti-Liberal Sunday, Anti-Moderate Sunday, and Anti-Fellow Fundamentalist Sunday.

For the Community Churches of Unlimited Possibilities, we suggest God Wants You to Have a Swimming Pool Sunday, How to Overcome Those Five-Figure Income Blues Sunday, God Wants You to Have Your Own Business Sunday, God Wants You to Have a Mercedes-Benz Sunday, Attaining Impossible Dreams Sunday, Climbing Steep Mountains Sunday, Running the Fastest Race Sunday, and Getting the Most Out of Life Sunday.

Then there are the Action Churches of the Relevant New World Order, for whom a number of possibilities suggest themselves: Anti-Nuke Sunday, Get Out of Central America Sunday, Anti-Multinational Sunday, Clean Air and Water Sunday, What's Wrong With the Moral Majority Sunday, Lay Down Your Weapons Sunday, WCC Sunday, NCC Sunday, May Day Sunday, and Grape-Pickers Sunday.

For the Jesus Saves Right Now Church, the possibilities are virtually endless: Fire and Brimstone Sunday, Jocks for Jesus Sunday, Singers for the Savior Sunday, Criminals for Christ Sunday, Midgets for Morality Sunday, Actresses for Submission Sunday, Buy Our 100th Bus Sunday, and Magic Pete and His Gospel Puppets Sunday.

Then there are the Churches of the Dispensational End-Time Prophecy, for which we suggest Abomination of Desolation Sunday, Armageddon is Near Sunday, Anti-Christ Identification Sunday, Certain Signs of the End Sunday, Are You Ready for the Rapture Sunday, Peril of the Universal Product Code Mark Sunday, Russia's Invasion of Israel Sunday, China's Invasion of Israel Sunday, Egypt's Invasion of Israel Sunday, and Arabia's Invasion of Israel Sunday.

Another possibility, of course, is to just preach through the Bible. 🔑

From Issue #90/April–May, 1986

AS THE PULPIT TURNS

By Doug Peterson

From Issue #90/April–May, 1986

The scene opens as the tall, handsome Giff Richards dons a pair of sunglasses and ducks into a small Catholic church where he meets with Father O'Steinberg.

GIFF: Father, we've got to stop meeting like this. My pastor is getting suspicious.

FATHER: Does this mean that you've made your decision?

GIFF: (Taking a breath) Yes, Father, I've finally decided to leave my Methodist church and become a Catholic.

FATHER: Well, I'm pleased that—
Suddenly, the music becomes ominous and a doctor rushes into the church with a look of urgency.

FATHER: If I'm not mistaken, you have a look of urgency, Dr. Boffkin.

DR. BOFFKIN: Yes, Father, I have terrible news for Mr. Richards here. Giff, your Methodist church just had a head-on collision with its national office, and it's in critical condition at the Burley Heights Hospital.

GIFF: What!!? Is my church going to die!?

DR. BOFFKIN: I doubt it. In cases like this, a church usually hangs on for about fifteen years, dangling near death, part blind . . . I'm sorry . . . so sorry.
The doctor leaves his bill and then dashes from the church. There is a long silence.

FATHER: (With a trembling voice) So how will this new twist of fate affect your decision? Will you still become a Catholic?

GIFF: I'm sorry, Father, but I changed my mind. I can't desert my church at a time like this. It needs me.

FATHER: But what about *me*!? Do you think I'm just your plaything—someone you can get your jollies with at weekday Mass and then leave all alone on Sunday mornings while you spend time with your Methodist church? Do you think our church doesn't have feelings?

GIFF: How can you say that, Father? I've been good to you.

FATHER: Oh sure, you buy me expensive overhead projectors and mink choir robes. But I want more than superficial signs of affection. I want you to be part of our family life here.

GIFF: You mean commitment?

FATHER: Yes, Gifford. Love. Do you know the meaning of that word?

GIFF: Of course. I play tennis.

Suddenly, tension fills the air.

FATHER: Giff, I don't know how to tell you this . . .

GIFF: Yes Father?

FATHER: Giff . . . I have your child.

GIFF: What!!?

FATHER: Yes, it's true. Your 10-year-old Timmy has been coming to learn catechism ever since we started giving away ice cream sundaes for every word that the children memorize.

GIFF: Oh, so that explains it. My wife and I were wondering what happens to Timmy every week. After excusing himself to go to the bathroom on Sunday mornings, he always comes back two hours later and twenty pounds heavier.

FATHER: Are you bitter, Giff?

GIFF: Of course not, Father. I just wish you didn't give Timmy so much ice cream. With his overeating, he's become so big that we had to hire a ground crew to pull a tarp over him whenever it rains.

FATHER: So, Gifford, what are you going to do now that you know about your child?

GIFF: (Knitting his brow and crocheting his nose) Father, I've changed my mind again. This time, I think I'm really going to do it. I'm going to tell my pastor that I'm leaving the Methodist church.

The scene fades out. Then it fades in to find tall, handsome Giff Richards with the pastor of a church from his distant past—a Lutheran church that Giff attended for a brief, impassioned summer. Giff and the pastor are talking at the bar of a crowded singles seminary.

REV. STOKES: Gifford, it's been a long time since we last talked . . . since you left me for that Episcopalian hussy.

GIFF: Yes, it's been a long time.

REV. STOKES: So why the reunion?

GIFF: I need advice on how to leave my Methodist church and join a Catholic congregation. I remembered that you always gave me good counsel when I was a member of your church.

REV. STOKES: Ah, so now the Methodists are getting the axe. Are you *really* going to commit yourself to the Catholic church, or are you just gonna live together? Giff, when will you ever learn that—?

GIFF: I didn't ask for a sermon! I simply need your advice!

REV. STOKES: OK, OK. (Smiling and looking off into the distance) Remember the good times we used to have, Giff? Remember the first time you signed our membership rolls and you knew it was love at first sight?

GIFF: Ah yes, those were the days.

REV. STOKES: (Bitterly) But then you started your series of one-Sunday stands! First it was a Baptist church! Then it was the Church of Christ. And then it was the Holy Shake and Shout Gospel Rock Church . . .

GIFF: That's not true! There was never anything between me and the Holy Shake and Shout Gospel Rock Church. I just fed their snakes every afternoon.

REV. STOKES: Maybe so, but I'll never forget the day that I came to your house unexpected and found an Episcopalian minister lurking behind the curtains with membership information in his hands! You two-timing scum!

GIFF: But everybody was doing it at the time! Sally and Bud Winkins used to check in at a remote Lutheran chapel and sign the guest book as Mr. and Mrs. Smith. Jim Collins used to make passes at Presbyterian churches and the Fickers used to attend church-swapping parties on a regular basis!

REV. STOKES: But that still

didn't make it right! After what you did to me, you have some nerve to think I'd advise you on how to leave your present church!

Rev. Stokes empties his glass in Gifford's face and storms from the bar. Irritated and gloomy, Giff drags his way toward the nearest door. But he pauses when he sees Dr. Boffkin sitting in the corner reading x-rays. Dr. Boffkin puts a bookmark in his x-rays and greets Gifford.

DR. BOFFKIN: Giff, I've been looking at your x-rays. Can we talk?

GIFF: What did you find, doc? You can be up front with me.

The doctor and Giff move up front in the bar. Then the doctor gives him the news.

" I had hoped we could part in friendship " said Giff

DR. BOFFKIN: Looking on the bright side, Giff, I can safely say that you'll be completely healthy for the rest of your life . . . all one minute of it.

GIFF: I only have one minute to live!?

DR. BOFFKIN: 56, 55, 54 . . .

GIFF: But what's wrong with me!?

DR. BOFFKIN: 51, 50, 49 . . . I'm sorry to say this, but you have a terminal case of pantophobia—the fear of everything.

GIFF: You can tell *that* from my x-rays?

DR. BOFFKIN: No. I made my diagnosis after learning that you're afraid to take showers unless a lifeguard is present.

GIFF: Is there a cure, doctor?

DR. BOFFKIN: Only one. You must do the thing that you are the most afraid of doing. Can you pinpoint that one most fearful thing?

GIFF: (Dramatically) Yes. And I'm going to face that fear . . . now! *Rushing directly to the hospital where his church has been placed on an artificial respirator, Giff greets his Methodist pastor, Rev. Jimbo.*

GIFF: I must talk to you, Rev. Jimbo. It's deadly urgent . . .

REV. JIMBO: What is it, Giff? You can be up front with me.

GIFF: No, I'd rather stand here and tell you. Rev. Jimbo, I . . . I . . . Gee, I'm trying to open up my heart to you, but I don't know how to begin.

REV. JIMBO: Would you like to learn? There's an open heart surgery in progress down the hall.

GIFF: No, Rev. Jimbo, I must tell you this *now*, even though it terrifies me to do so. I must tell you that . . . I'm . . . I'm seeing another church.

REV. JIMBO: (Falling back into a chair) What!? Are you telling me that you're having an extramenical affair!?

GIFF: I didn't want it to happen . . . but when I met a new church and my heart told me that this was Rev. Right, what could I do?

REV. JIMBO: So who is it!? Is it some young church with guitar services? Or is it that trendy church where the deaconesses print the names of their Bible study groups on the bottoms of their sweat pants?

GIFF: It's a Catholic church, Rev. Jimbo.

REV. JIMBO: Papist! I should have suspected this on the night you came home with incense on your collar. So why did you choose this moment to tell me? Our church is in critical condition!

GIFF: Please don't get angry. I'm just trying to be honest.

REV. JIMBO: Since when are *you* honest! You're the one who got away with murder as our church treasurer until someone read the annual report and discovered that half of our funds were listed under "Majestic Stride, to win in the fifth."

GIFF: How was I to guess that someone would really read the annual report!?

REV. JIMBO: I suppose you want custody of your tithe.

GIFF: Of course. But don't worry, Rev. Jimbo, I'd be happy to give you visiting rights to my wallet every other weekend.

There is a long pause.

REV. JIMBO: So what was it, Giff? Did you start fooling around because you didn't like our Sunday School program?

GIFF: No, that wasn't it . . . although I admit I wasn't too thrilled with the time you had a Navy tattoo artist put Biblical scenes on the backs of all the kids.

REV. JIMBO: Yes, you're right. That was a mistake.

GIFF: But my problems went deeper than that. I was . . . I was just bored.

REV. JIMBO: Bored!? Is that all!? You were just bored and wanted a change!? What do you think a church is—just another consumer product that you discard when you've used it up!?

GIFF: Now don't get self-righteous with me, Rev. Jimbo! You encourage a consumer mentality as much as anyone! Didn't you just start running a TV ad that claims our church absorbs more sins than the other leading brand!?

REV. JIMBO: Yes, but that's different. I . . . I . . .

Rev. Jimbo breaks down in tears.

GIFF: I'm sorry. I didn't mean to hurt you. I'm always saying the wrong things. I was always a bad communicator in our relationship.

REV. JIMBO: Yes, but that's mainly because you were afraid of using nouns in your sentences. (Wiping away tears) But now . . . now you're cured.

GIFF: Yes, I am, aren't I?

REV. JIMBO: And you're also excommunicated from the church softball league. I'll see to that.

GIFF: I had hoped we could part in friendship.

REV. JIMBO: How can I remain friends with the one who broke my heart?

Rev. Jimbo blows his nose, gives a parting glance at Gifford and walks sadly away. Gifford sighs, wipes a tear from his eye and leaves through a rear exit.

ANNOUNCER: So what will become of tall, handsome Giff Richards? Will he try to make something of his commitment to the Catholic church? Or will his head continue to be turned by every vestment that passes by? Will he bring his finicky passions under control? Or will he soon be unfaithful to the Catholic church and begin attending the Pentecostal fellowship that he's had his eye on?

Tune in tomorrow for another episode of . . . (Dramatic music) . . . *As The Pulpit Turns.*

Roll credits. Fade out.

Truth Is Stranger Than Fiction

Go to church, get a dollar

ROCHESTER, N.Y. (AP) — A Lutheran church will cast its bread upon the parishioners Sunday.

Churchgoers will be paid a dollar for their troubles when they arrive for services.

"We wanted to try something different," said Lawrence Luescher, vice president of the church council of the Lutheran Church of Peace and a retired advertising man.

One Susan B. Anthony silver dollar will be given to every man, woman and child, "visitors and members alike," who shows up for the service, Luescher said in an interview Thursday.

"We think that's going to attract some people to the church who have never been there before," he said. "Hopefully, they will like our service enough to attend another Sunday and maybe eventually join the church."

ABOVE: From Issue #63/December, 1981–January, 1982; RIGHT: From Issue #45/October–November, 1978; BELOW: From Issue #34/December, 1976–January, 1977

Pastor's subject for Sunday, Oct. 16
11 a.m.

The Five Worst Sinners in Dayton, Tenn.

Their Names and Who They Are

Westside Baptist Church

HWY. 30 WEST • DAYTON, TENN.

Sunday School . . . . 10:00 a.m.
Morning Worship . . . . 11:00 a.m.
Training Union . . . . 6:00 p.m.
Evening Worship . . . . 6:30 p.m.
Wed. Prayer Service. . . . . . 7:00 p.m.

PASTOR - TOMMY LOCKWOOD
ASSISTANT PASTOR - WALLY GILMER

HWY. 30 WEST • DAYTON, TENN.

RELIGIOUS IRONY, DEPT.

REWARD

A REWARD OF $100.00 WILL BE PAID FOR INFORMATION LEADING TO THE ARREST AND CONVICTION OF THE PERSON OR PERSONS RESPONSIBLE FOR REMOVING THE CHURCH OF CHRIST SIGN FROM ITS LOCATION AT THE JUNCTION OF WALTON FERRY ROAD AND LUNA LANE. ALL INFORMATION SHOULD BE REPORTED TO THE HENDERSONVILLE POLICE.

LOVE AND MERCY CHURCH OF CHRIST

LAKESIDE PARK ELEMENTARY SCHOOL
PHONE 824-6945

(From the Hendersonville, Tennessee "Star News")

T.I.S.T.F.

A cool Sunday

Members of Grassland Heights Baptist Church were relieved to see this sign at the church on Hillsboro Rd.

Will swop pastoral services (wedding, baptism, funeral) or Victorian oak bed for bird's-eye maple full-sized bed, preferably turn of the century. F 701 PA

LEFT: From Issue #69/October–November, 1982; ABOVE: From Issue #106/July–August, 1989; BELOW: From Issue #78/April–May, 1984

Teen struck by lightning in church

By Roberta Helman
Press Staff Reporter

Nineteen-year-old John Dauble admits he left church services yesterday with a "bad case of nerves."

He left in an ambulance — after being knocked from his chair onto the floor when hit by a bolt of lightning.

Worship services at Our Saviour Lutheran Church had started only moments before when, as young Dauble describes it, "all of a sudden I saw sparks under my feet."

There was a loud boom, and he was on the floor.

Rev. Joel Vogel, pastor of the East Side church at 6501 Madison, said the lightning created a ball of fire that hit in three places, knocking bricks out of an exterior wall and knocking out the organ and amplification system.

Young Dauble, apparently all right today, was the only one injured among the more than 100 persons attending the 11 a.m. service.

He was assisted immediately by another church member, Dr. Ray Nicholson Jr., who is Dauble's family doctor. Smiling about the incident today, he said he spent the remainder of yesterday resting, with a "case of nerves."

"What was really unusual," he added, "was that it happened when my minister, my doctor and my family were all there."

John is the son of Mr. and Mrs. Gerald Dauble of 1041 Rosemarie and a student at University of Evansville. He said when the lightning struck, he had just sat down in a chair at the rear of the church and leaned his wet head against a metal strip between two windows.

73

The forgotten addiction

or 'Why are Snickerdoodles so Critical at Church Functions?'

By James F. Sennett

From Issue #84/April–May, 1985

We've come full circle. In the 1960s, we rebelled against all the communicated, traditional American values. We even replaced old vices with new ones. We shunned the alcohol of the middle class to dare the illicit charms of grass, acid, and speed. We were right to point out that one vice was no worse than another. But collectively, we ignored the fact that all contribute to physical, emotional, and sociological ruin.

And now the revolution is dead. While the heavy users have traded their eight-way sunshine and Acapulco Gold for free-based coke and 'ludes, a new generation with alligator shirts and $100 sneakers has discovered that—with no cause behind them—the controlled goodies are just expensive thrills. So they have rediscovered alcohol: cheaper, legal, and oh, so available. Goodbye, Timothy Leary. Hello, Jack Daniels.

It's a complete cycle of escape. Yet, through it all, a quiet, unassuming, deadly addiction holds our nation and our Church by the throat—passing unnoticed by the millions who otherwise are socially aware and concerned. I speak of the insurmountable problem of food addiction.

Oh, sure, there is great news in eating disorders. Become anorexic or bulimic and you will have the local ace reporters stumbling over themselves to get an exclusive. Or lose two hundred pounds, buy orange tights, and perfect a Lou Sayers impression and you will have a television contract before you can say, "Blow it out."

But what about the basic slob who cannot stop after three Oreo cookies and who doesn't feel secure until he has stuffed himself sick? No one rushes to do human-interest side bars about three-hundred-pound food junkies. No one seems to care about the special miseries suffered by victims of this forgotten addiction.

Mainly, unfat people believe that there is no real problem here—only a lack of basic self-control and personal pride. The great myth about overeaters is, "They could lose weight if they really wanted to." Well, I *really* wanted to for over ten years. I went from two hundred forty pounds to three hundred fifty pounds, and I hated myself every step of the way. In a culture that calls alcoholism a disease and spends millions to rehabilitate those destroyed by the gods of the pillbox, there is very little sympathy and very little patience for the helpless addict drowning in his own body fat.

There are the token AA spin-offs for chronic overeaters—and one cannot make it through the average newspaper or situation comedy without encountering several fool-proof plans to lose 30 percent of your body weight by the next full moon. But these are mostly faddish, sensational, and unproductive. For every "I lost seventy-five pounds and eight inches," there are dozens of "I went to three meetings and dropped out for a hot fudge sundae." Of course, there are legitimate programs run by concerned people, which make significant progress. But these are far too scarce. And those helped are but a "chosen few." There is, yet, no national conscience, no social mandate to offer consolation and genuine help for those who strangle their vital organs in excess weight.

Rest assured, we are dealing with full-fledged addiction here. My doctor friends, who know about this sort of thing, tell me that the body becomes addicted to sugars and carbohydrates and other empty-calorie villains the same way it does to alcohol, nicotine, or narcotics. There is a dependency on these substances—physical and psychological—which leads to very familiar behavior patterns. At the height of my addiction, I lied about my eating. I pigged out by myself. I spent money designated for other vital purposes on junk food. I ate until I was stuffed. Then I waited for my stomach to make more room and I ate again.

If this behavior pattern had only involved liquor, rather than food, I would have been diagnosed "alcoholic"—then I would have become the recipient of all the patience and care afforded the victim of a socially acceptable behavioral disorder. But since my problem was eating, I was merely "written off" as one with no self-discipline and no will power,

one who didn't care about himself, his family, or his God. I cared. I cared as much then as I do now—four suit sizes smaller. But I was caught in a trap of uncontrollable behavior. I wept for the lack of someone who would guide me rather than goad me, who would pray with me rather than preach to me, who would understand my pain rather than understate my plight.

There is one aspect of addiction, which actually makes the chronic overeater worse off than the doper, the drunk, or the smokestack. These other substances can generally be overcome with a short, intense "cold turkey" session. In fact, that is often the most effective therapy. At least the behavior patterns can be broken. Then the addict can take steps to totally divorce himself from the substance itself and the world which encouraged his problem.

But this remedy is not available to the overeater. One cannot choose to stop eating. The task to be performed is to go from eating too much to eating just enough. But in overeating, as in alcoholism, it is always easier not to start than it is to stop. Telling a compulsive/obsessive overeater that he must eat so much and stop is tantamount to telling an alcoholic he must have one and only one drink three times a day. I trust you can appreciate the insurmountable task this presents for one who is subconsciously driven to the refrigerator as others are to the bottle or the hypodermic needle.

I do not begrudge the victims of alcohol, tobacco, or drugs, their "acceptable addiction" status. Were it not for such social awareness and eagerness to help, millions of people would continue to kill themselves with no possible way to escape. We do well to love them with the love of our Lord. But I do issue a Church-wide call to reach out to the millions of chronic food abusers who need our love and compassion as much as any of the others. There are some radical steps that will need to be taken if this avenue of ministry is to be explored.

First, many "good Christians" (including a significant number of pastors) will have to admit that they, too, are addicts. There is a strange schizophrenia regarding overeating in the Church, which condemns gluttony as sin and yet allows fat Christians unchallenged status in the Spiritual Giants Hall of Fame. If compulsive overeating is accepted as a behavior disorder in need of our attention, many will have to admit that they are in sin and need the help of brothers and sisters to overcome it. This is pretty radical stuff—smacking of relational theology and honesty in communication. It may be easier to nod at the problem in the third person and keep our walls and masks in place.

We will also have to reorganize an entire social sub-structure within the Church. The aforementioned schizophrenia allows us to despise overeaters and yet take every opportunity to shove food (rich, sticky, sweet, icky food) under their noses. One day, we will wake up to the fact that Christians don't have to be eating to get along with each other. Count the Church functions you attend in one month where fattening, empty-calorie food is available and pushed. We not only feed the habits of those already hooked, we daily create new food junkies with our immoral gluttony feasts. No wonder so many preachers have weight problems. They have to go to all these functions—where people are offended if they don't delight over the cream puffs, barbecued spare ribs, and rhubarb pie.

Anyone who would wave a bottle under an alcoholic's nose, or force a full shot glass into his hand, would be considered among history's greatest cads. But we constantly surround the calorie addict with irresistible temptations, then piously exclaim, "It's not my fault if he can't control himself." The next time the education committee meets, or the local Bible College sends a singing group around, try ice water, prayer, and edifying conversation for refreshments. No one will miss the snickerdoodles. And maybe someone will grow up instead of out.

But mainly we must be ready to counsel, share, and be present with those who suffer this sin problem. We must decide that overeating *is* an addiction; it is a complicated emotional, physical, and spiritual disorder which can only be dealt with through discipleship and support. I am currently being saved (eighty-one pounds down, seventy-plus to go) through the concerted efforts of a whole network of supportive, loving believers who expect no miracles, but applaud every progressive baby step. And it all began with one man—fortunately a physician—who decided I was worth helping and who has spent many hours listening to me and giving me wise counsel. He never preached to me or made me feel guilty in any way. He knows that I have enough guilt to last a lifetime and it's gotten me nowhere.

Of course, the solution is complicated. The problem is hopelessly complicated. But we serve a complicated God—one who is able to untie any Gordian knot and solve the most perplexing riddles of life. And His solution for universal sin lies in a Church bound to a Savior and dedicated to one another. If we commit ourselves to our brothers and sisters with overeating addictions, we can find God-given solutions and erase yet another blot of inconsistency and apathy from the record of the saints.

From Issue #72/April–May, 1983

From Issue #103/June–July, 1988

A *young man* approaches a woman seated behind a desk . . . .

By Dinah Stokes

From Double Issue #98 & 99/August–September–
October–November, 1987

Man: I'm inquiring about your Bible study classes. Do you have anything I can attend on
Tuesday nights?

Woman: I'm sorry, sir, but that Bible study is for
married couples, ages forty to fifty.

Man: How about Wednesdays?

Woman: No, Wednesdays are reserved for the
newly divorced, under age thirty-eight,
who work full-time.

Man: Well, why don't you just read the schedule
to me.

Woman: Certainly!
Thursdays, it's the Formerly Engaged
Bible Study. They're studying Lamenta-
tions.
Friday evenings, the over-80's meet, al-
though attendance has been slipping. Late
Friday (3 to 4 A.M. Saturday, actually) the
Hard Rock group gets together to read
Matthew, Mark, Luke, and Elton John.
Saturday afternoons, the Yuppie Bible
Study group meets (usually right after they
run); they're into "From Corinthians to
Cuisinarts."
We still have some room available in
either the "Working thru Mid-life Crisis"
Bible Study group on Mondays or the "PC
Owners User-Friendly" Bible Study group.
Do you have the New Testament on floppy
disk?

Man: (Turning away, then back) Maybe I'll just
watch Dr. Ogilvie on television.

Woman: Good idea!

79

The Wittenburg

DARE!

From Issues #78, 105, 106, 109

Some of the strangest goings-on within the Church have been documented in a regular Door feature known as "The Wittenburg Dare." In this feature, readers are dared to send in various items . . . anything from photographs of ugly cars owned by pastors to stories of weird interruptions during church services.

The request for "weird interruptions of a church service" worked particularly well, eliciting stories such as these:

• While a guest speaker was giving a sermon one Sunday, his pants suddenly fell to his ankles. But since the podium was large, the speaker kept on talking. Only the choir, which sat behind the podium, had a good view of the disaster. As the person telling this story noted, "To their eternal glory, only one lady had to leave the service."

• During a wedding ceremony, a guy suddenly barged into the church pulling a pregnant woman with him and shouting, "Stop the wedding! You can't let this go on! Look what Manuel did to my sister!" When the pastor calmly said, "There's no Manuel here," the fellow glanced around and declared, "Oh no! Wrong wedding!" Then he left.

• In the middle of a service, a man abruptly shot up from his chair and shouted, "Thus saith the Lord thy God, 'Gather thy chickens . . . '" After a pause, he said "Excuse me" and sat down.

• While a certain minister was giving a sermon, the lights in the church suddenly went out for about a minute or two. After the service, the minister asked what had happened, only to discover that it had nothing to do with the church's electrical system. A prominent woman in the church had simply asked the head usher to turn off the lights so she could see if her dried flower arrangement glowed in the dark.

• During a fiery sermon on our power over evil, a two-foot-long snake slithered down the aisle, coming straight for the preacher. The preacher proceeded to stomp the creature to bits, just before a fourteen-year-old boy entered the church and screamed, "You killed my snake!!"

• One Sunday, a minister stood before the pulpit and didn't say a word for what seemed like an eternity. Finally, he asked, "Does anyone have a good joke?" When nobody responded, he went home.

• During one of his first wedding ceremonies at a new church, a pastor had to put up with the brother-in-law of the bride, who was taking photographs like crazy. Even during prayer, flash-bulbs were popping. While debating whether it would be inappropriate to stop his prayer and tell the guy to cut it out, the minister peeked open his eyes. What he saw was the brother-in-law climbing on top of a covered baptistery to get a better angle on the service. Before the minister could shout, "Look out!" the brother-in-law reached the top and crashed through. As the pastor put it, "The shouted 'I'll sue,' coming from the depths of a deep baptistery linger on as the funniest words spoken by a newly immersed convert."

• In the middle of a barn-burner of a sermon, a preacher opened his mouth wide, only to suddenly start choking and gagging and coughing. After falling to the floor behind the pulpit, the minister continued to choke. Finally, his red face reappeared above the pulpit and he desperately explained, "You won't . . . choke, choke . . . believe it . . . cough, cough . . . but I just . . . choke, cough . . . swallowed a fly!"

• After giving a half-hour sermon, a minister decided to leave the service because he was terribly bothered by his cold. He wanted to clear his nose without disturbing the solemnity of the service, but there was one big problem. He was still wearing his cordless microphone. As a result, the entire congregation was treated to the extremely amplified sound of the minister blowing his nose and then discussing vacation plans with a church member.

One last note on the Wittenburg Dare. If you've just started a new church, and you're trying to come up with a name (something more exciting than "First Church of _____"), check out the Dare in Issue #105. Readers were asked to send in strange names of actual churches, and this is what they uncovered:

Lovers Lane United Methodist Church

Ralph Lutheran

Looney Valley Lutheran

Fertile Lutheran

Happy Church

International House of Philoxenia

Dolly Pond Church of God in Grasshopper Settlement

Mitchell Chapel Church of the Fire Baptized Holiness Church of God of the Americas

Country Club Christian Church

Catholic Church of South Africa King George Win the War

Light Pink Baptist Church

The Church of the Big Hole

Some Good Ol' American
MEMORY
VERSES

Just the way we remember them . . .

By Den Hart

From Issue #79/June–July, 1984

"Be not conformed to this world, but be transformed by the renewing of your MasterCard" — ROMANS 12:2

"Another man, one of His disciples, said to Him, 'Lord, first let me go and bury my father.' And Jesus told him, 'OK. No problem—it's just as well that you do that right now—I mean, I wouldn't want to inconvenience anyone.'" — MATTHEW 8:21

"Put to death, therefore, whatever belongs to your earthly nature: sexual immorality, impurity, lust, evil desires and greed, which is idolatry. Clothe yourselves, therefore, in successful business ventures, a good self-image, polyesters, and a deep tan." — COLOSSIANS 3:5

"If a brother sins against you, go and tell someone else, but don't approach the brother about it. If he sins against you again, go and tell another person. And if he sins yet again, mention it to someone else, then drop a hint to the brother. Sooner or later they'll get the message. If not, leave the church and find somewhere else to go." — MATTHEW 18:5

"'Teacher,' he asked, 'what must I do to inherit eternal life?' He answered, 'Love the Lord your God with all your emotions, neglecting your mind, and love yourself first or you can't begin to love others.'" — LUKE 10:25-27

"When Jesus heard this, He said to him, ''You still lack one thing—sell all you possess and give to the poor . . . ha,ha, just kidding." — LUKE 18:22

"And now these three remain: faith, hope, and love. But the greatest of these is tongues." — 1 CORINTHIANS 13:13

"I'D JUST LIKE TO REAFFIRM MY PLEDGE TO NOT TRIM MY MUSTACHE UNTIL ALL THE MONEY IS RAISED."

ABOVE: From Issue #108/
November–December, 1989;
RIGHT: From Issue #49/June–July, 1979;
BELOW: From Issue #86/
August–September, 1985

"Mr. Voorman? . . . You filled out a 'Visitor' card at First-Christian last Sunday morning, Hmm?. . ."

5

The Hollow Part on the Inside of Your Leg Right Behind the Knee

Social and Political Issues

You know about reflex reactions, don't you? That's when the body needs to respond to something real quick and bypasses the brain to do it. It just responds without consulting anybody—kind of like our country's foreign policy.

One of our oldest reflex actions is the "fight or flight" response. The theory goes like this: When a primitive man was attacked by a fierce creature, his reflexes told him to either fight or run away. Modern people, being more sophisticated than cave people, have developed a third reflex action. When we are attacked, we either fight, run away, or take the person to court. Then we wait six years for a judge to hear our case, by which time the person threatening us is either bored, senile, or dead.

All of this is a great lead-in to our discussion of that hollow part on the inside of your leg right behind the knee where a bunch of muscles connect—muscles that control one of the most famous reflex actions of all. The knee-jerk reaction.

You've seen this demonstrated in comedy sketches in which the doctor taps the patient's knee, causing the patient's foot to shoot up and smash the doctor's face. Then the doctor files a "mal-patient" lawsuit, which is tied up in court for at least six years, by which time they are all either bored, senile, or dead.

Knee-jerk reactions are well-known in the political sphere as well. Conservatives have built-in reflexes that cause them to react conservatively to just about every issue on earth—always with the right knee, of course, while liberals have a left-knee version.

Thanks to the knee-jerk reaction, we see glaring inconsistencies on both sides of the political knee. Conservatives claim that all life is sacred, except when national security requires us to threaten an entire country with annihilation from nuclear warheads. Liberals get into a righteous tizzy protecting the life of a rare species of snail, but are shocked at the idea that it might be wrong to end the life of an unborn human child.

The Door, of course, is immune to knee-jerk reactions (although there is some evidence that it specializes in just plain "jerk" reactions).

However, I don't want to leave the impression that instinctive responses are always wrong. A built-in, instinctive response to injustice is crucial for our moral survival. Take the reaction to discrimination, for example. It's a healthy, vital reflex.

In 1984, *The Door* tested this important response by discriminating against its readers. They did this by making the issue on racism (#77) look like the rough layout had simply been photocopied and sent out to certain subscribers. A note on the cover explained that "due to a shortage of printed issues, we have sent this photocopy of the rough layouts to you and others like you." Then a note on the inside said that the editors had considered photocopying one of the finished, printed issues, rather than photocopying the rough layout, but decided against that plan because they were in a hurry to get those finished copies in the mail to "our other customers."

One reader wrote back saying, "I was appalled when I received a photocopied issue in the mail, and you didn't even have the decency to apologize!"

Another said, "You have the brazen impudence to state

under 'Further Explanation' you needed to get all those (printed copies) in the mail to your customers. So what am I . . . chopped liver?"

Another added, "I have legal doubts about your sending photocopied magazines to someone such as I, who paid for a subscription that was to be finished and printed."

Another pointed out the bigotry of sending photocopies to less-deserving subscribers, another threatened to cancel her subscription, and another asked, "You *were* kidding about running out of copies, right? I should hope so . . . although, the Xerox copy was actually one of your more attractive issues."

I'm happy to report that the reflex response to discrimination is in fine working order. I'm also happy to report that *The Door* makes a pretty good hammer, tapping on our knees and testing our reflexes. So let's tap away at a few social and political issues—like racism, feminism, and nuclear bombism. 🔑

Please read me the part where Curious George confounds the civil authorities with wit and cunning only to find himself inescapably entwined in a complex ethical dilemna over the appropriateness of eating bananas imported from economically oppressed countries . . .

From Issue #75/October–November, 1983

From Issue #68/August–September, 1982

GROUND ZERO:Wheaton

The effects of a 20-megaton bomb Detonated at ground level Billy Graham Center, Wheaton, Ill.

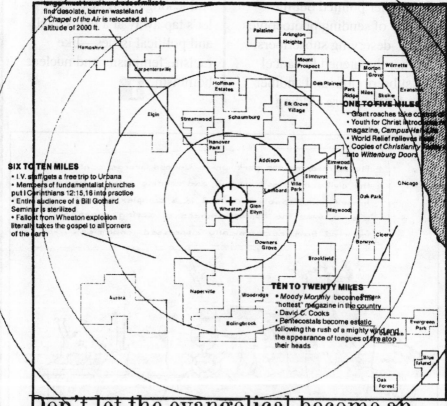

GROUND ZERO TO ONE MILE
- All Wheaton students are charred black, trustees panic and start lowering property values
- Christian Camping International no longer must travel hundreds of miles to find desolate, barren wasteland
- *Chapel of the Air* is relocated at an altitude of 2000 ft.

ONE TO FIVE MILES
- Giant roaches take control of the NAE
- Youth for Christ introduces new magazine, *Campus Half Life*
- World Relief relieves itself
- Copies of *Christianity Today* mutate into *Wittenburg Doors*

SIX TO TEN MILES
- I.V. staff gets a free trip to Urbana
- Members of fundamentalist churches put I Corinthians 12:15,16 into practice
- Entire audience of a Bill Gothard Seminar is sterilized
- Fallout from Wheaton explosion literally takes the gospel to all corners of the earth

TEN TO TWENTY MILES
- *Moody Monthly* becomes the "hottest" magazine in the country
- David C. Cooks
- Pentecostals become estatic following the rush of a mighty wind and the appearance of tongues of fire atop their heads

Don't let the evangelical become an endangered species, BAN THE BOMB

—Kraig Klaudt

How Safe are Nuclear Families?
Community Christmas Cookies

Here's Justice America

Sobouring

December
1979

The Politics of Santa:
The Justification of Fat

Pages 89–92 From Issue #51/October–November 1979

Here's Justice America

Jim Walrus, Founder and
President Sobouring
International

During last week's march on the Key Bridge Baskin-Robbins ice cream store, God gave me a vision for America: Liberty to the Captives and Justice for All by Groundhog Day, 1980.

I knew it would be a monumental assignment, with a tremendous amount of pain and suffering ahead, but I cheerfully accepted the task because I happen to enjoy pain and suffering. Already we have mobilized tens of thousands of student demonstrators all over this continent and we are expecting tens of thousands more as "Here's Justice, America" is launched in major cities all across this nation. Volunteers are being trained at beautiful Arrowhead Slums, our international headquarters, and then being sent out by the tens of thousands with black arm bands which read "I've had it!"

Our *Sobouring* printing presses are turning out millions of booklets with the "Four Radical Principles" for distribution. The Four Radical Principles were my idea (copyright 1979 by Jim Walrus, All Rights Reserved) and neatly sum up the whole council of God this way:

Principle One: God loves the poor and oppressed and has a radical Cause for your life. (Matt. 25:32-46)

Principle Two: Man is unjust, rich, powerful, capitalistic, and militaristic; therefore, he is separated from God and cannot know and experience God's Cause. (Matt. 25:32-46)

Principle Three: Identification with the poor and the oppressed is God's ONLY provision for this injustice and tyranny, and only through active involvement with suffering brothers and sisters can we know and experience God's Cause for our lives. (Matt. 25:32-46)

Principle Four: We must corporately stand up to the principalities and powers, demonstrate in the highways and byways, boycott grapes and Nestle's Quick, and subscribe to Sobouring magazine, receiving it into our homes or offices each month. Then we can know and experience God's Cause for our lives. (Matt. 25:32-46)

Only yesterday I was on a plane, returning from one of my many speaking engagements, when I asked a man sitting next to me if he had ever heard of the Four Radical Principles. He was dressed conservatively in a suit and tie, and looked as if he might have, at one time, had a thin mustache.

The man quickly pulled out a little booklet of his own and said, "No, but have you heard of the Four Spiritual Laws?" to which I replied, "Hey, who are you anyway? Haven't I seen you somewhere before?" By then he was trying to get me to pray a little prayer that was printed on the last page of his booklet, but I grabbed it out of his hand, ripped it up, and stuffed it into the seat pocket in front of me.

He then pressed his stewardess call button and asked for another seat, but I threw myself across the aisle to block his exit and to symbolically protest

(continued on page 10)

A Day in Siberia

A warm reminder from a cold place

When Jim Walrus, founder and president of Sobouring, asked me to travel to a small village in Russia to report firsthand on conditions there, I was concerned. Concerned that the CIA-dominated customs agency would not allow me to travel to Russia, and concerned that the capitalistic, pig American government would not allow an objective report. After six months of harassment by the fascist State Department, I was allowed to fly to the village of Rylpvck, a small worker's cooperative in Siberia.

Our tiny Russian plane landed in Rylpvck early on a Monday morning. It was the middle of winter and the temperature was a pleasant 30 below zero. I could see the workers in the field happily pounding the frozen dirt. The simple outline of the cooperative housing made my heart jump with anticipation. I felt embarrassed as I emerged from the plane with my symbols of materialism—Levis, short-sleeved shirt, and Adidas tennis shoes. I also felt stupid as I stood there frozen in the doorway of the plane unable to move. I had forgotten my jacket. While I was thawing out by the quaint wood stove inside the small airport office, I met my hosts, Wanda and Ed Kzyvkskyvosknishanyvesknineynkov. They didn't speak English and I didn't speak Russian, but I could tell by the twinkle in their eyes and the compassionate smiles on their faces, they were happy. Happier than any Americans I had ever seen.

We walked slowly to their farm. I remember my feelings as they pointed to their little one-room cooperative house and said, "Dumpski." Tears welled up in my eyes. They obviously were very proud. Later, as we sat on the ice floor, Ed looked intently in my eyes and said, "Getyov usky outnoy ofwek here." I didn't understand a word he was saying, but it was obviously a message to the American people. A plea for simplicity. A call back to the richness of living close to nature. I put my arm around him and said, "I understand, I understand." Both Ed and Wanda looked at each other and then repeated over and over, "Idioski, idioski"—obviously an untranslatable folkism.

They looked so healthy. I asked them to show me their farm. They took me outside to the shed and I could sense that these were people of the earth. They worked with their hands. And then Ed and Wanda showed me the tools the government had given them to work the 2,000 acres that were theirs—primitive, yes, but if you could have seen them as they held up the tools, tears streaming down their faces crying, "Thesy toolski are crapka," you would have celebrated with them their closeness to nature. I hugged them and again they chanted, "Idioski, idioski." Truly words that needed no translation. Words of liberation. Words of happiness.

I felt honored as they led me back into the house to eat with them. It was the first time I had eaten frozen soup, apparently a tradition in Siberia. As we ate, you could hear nothing but the chewing of ice and then, as we chipped frozen bread together, I could not help but think that this is what life is all about. I smiled at them. Then they grabbed my arm chanting, "Idioski, idioski. Thiski is the pitski"—a Russian poem, no doubt. I wanted to stay longer, but schedules have their limitations and I felt a certain urgency to communicate to my own "comrades," as it were, the deep sense of direction and inspiration given to me by these simple people. (continued on page 32)

Bouquet of Bombs

Pick some for your baby,
your little girl,
And your lady,
Pick some flowers for your granny
Before the grannies are all gone
From the bombs
  the bombs
   the bombs.

If they drop the bombs on Dallas
Or on our Washington palace,
I'll grab my young son Habakkuk,
My Bible, typewriter and
  Muckalucks,
And run into the
Civil Defense Shelter on 43rd Street
To escape the bombs
  the bombs
   the bombs.

by Jeff

PSALM 2023

The Bomb is my shepherd.
I shall proliferate.
It maketh me lie down in
    nuclear pastures;
It leadeth me beside bubbling
    waters.
It annihilates my soul:
It guideth me in the paths of
    radioactiveness
For its name sake.

Yea, though I walk through the
    valley of the shadow of the
    MX,
I will fear no evil; for I have
    Tridents too.
Its rads and its ICBM's, they
    comfort me;
It prepareth a nuclear umbrella
    before me in the presence of
    mine enemies.
It hath anointed my head with
    power and terror;
My cup melts down.
Surely fears and intimidation
    will precede me all the days
    of my half-life.
And I dwell in the rubble of the
    Bomb forever.
        — By Erik C. Nelson

From Issue #68/August–September, 1982

COLD WAR
HOME VERSION

Megatons of Fun for the Entire Family!

FROZEN OUT OF THE COLD WAR?

Ever feel that you are an insignificant part of global politics? That the nuclear arms race is too distant and impersonal? Does it bother you not to know a real communist? If so, then here's your opportunity to take part in the Cold War on a more humane, personal level.

IMAGINE, YOUR VERY OWN RUSSIAN ENEMY

That's right! We assign you a Soviet family just like your own. Together, you can escalate to any level of tension and hostility you desire. Mail threatening letters, spread nasty rumors, have 100 pizzas sent to their house . . . and send them the bill!

YOU HAVE YOUR OWN NUCLEAR WARHEAD

It's almost too good to be true. As soon as hostilities reach a fever pitch you can launch your own RON-CO family-size warhead at them. But be careful! They can always do the same to you!

Here's What You Get!

- Name and address of your very own real Russian family you can exchange hostilities with
- A CIA profile of things that make them mad
- Russian translation of a Don Rickles insult book so you can rank on their hockey teams, ugly women, space program and collective living. For example, try this one on them:

"Hey Ivan, does your wife shave her back before she goes to the beach?"

- Addresses of families in Central America and Asia that will host you and your Russian pen-pal should you ever want to tangle in person
- Water balloons, rubber band guns, spit wad shooters and banana cream pies for limited warfare
- Two tactical warheads for household use only
- Five miniature Polaris missiles to be hidden in your swimming pool
- Red, white and blue curtains for your window of vulnerability
- Home version of MX missile game. One member of the family must be hidden in a clothes hamper at all times. Clothes hampers not included
- Your own dartboard complete with photos of your Russian family and Yuri Andropov

Kraig Klaudt
From Issue #68/August–September, 1982

From Issue #77/February–March, 1984

HAZARDS AND

HOT WATER

By William H. Willimon

From Issue #70/December, 1982–January, 1983

One of the hazards of serving a church in Greenville, South Carolina, is that one has to put up with the presence of Bob Jones University— "The World's Most Unusual University." When Bishop Tullis moved me to Greenville, my friends said they would give me six months before I would be in hot water with the folks at Dr. Bob's school.

In scarcely three months, I had already had my first tiff with them over their dispute with the Internal Revenue Service. It seems that the IRS wanted to take away Dr. Bob's tax-exempt status be-

cause he had rules against interracial dating among his students. Ironically, I said that this was none of the IRS's business. It is not up to the tax people to judge what is a "valid religious belief." I simply said, in an interview with the *Greenville News*, that the IRS ought to lay off the good Dr. Jones.

"This is a free country," I said. "The Constitution guarantees that anybody can make a fool out of himself in the name of religion and get away with it. If Dr. Jones wants to give us Christians a bad name because of his racist attitudes, that's our problem, not the government's."

It seems that Dr. Jones was neither amused nor gratified by my support. In one of his evening chapel talks on his radio station, he called me "a liar, a liberal, a Communist, and an apostate." That's gratitude for you. A few weeks later, when Dr. Bob called upon the Lord to "smite Alexander Haig, hip and thigh," I decided not to have anything else to say about Dr. Jones or his racist school—he plays dirty.

One of my church members, upon hearing that Dr. Jones had labeled me an "apostate," said, "We suspected our preacher of being a Democrat but I didn't know anything about him being an 'apostate.' Is that some kind of perversion?" With as little theology as we Methodists have to start with, it is tough for us to become apostates. At any rate, this was the setting of a telephone call which I received about a week after Dr. Jones called me dirty names in his sermon.

Him: Hello, Dr. Willimon? This is Dean So-and-So of Bob Jones University. How are you tonight?

Me: Fine. At least I think I am.

Him: Good. Dr. Willimon, I was interested in your remarks about our school in the newspaper recently. I gathered, from reading your remarks, that you may not know much about our school. Perhaps you don't understand our programs, our goals.

Me: Possibly. However, I was born in Greenville, lived here most of my life, so I have followed Dr. Jones and his machinations for many years. I may know more about him than you do.

Him: Well, er, uh, that may be but, Dr. Willimon, can we have a Christian-to-Christian talk?

Me: I can.

Him: Now Dr. Willimon, you believe in the Bible don't you.

Me: I certainly do.

Him: Of course. Well, Bob Jones University is founded and operated on strictly Biblical principles. Take, for instance, our policies on the mixing of the races.

Me: Yes, let's take them.

Him: Well, they are based on strictly Biblical principles, on Biblical teaching.

Me: I doubt that. I expect that they are based on Dr. Jones' personal opinions of what is right—as are many of your rules there.

Him: Now look here. (Pause.) Dr. Willimon, you have a family?

Me: Yes I do.

Him: Do you have a daughter?

(At this point, I knew what was coming. After all, I wasn't born and bred in South Carolina for nothing.)

Me: I do.

Him: Well, how would you like for your own daughter to marry a black man?

Me: I wouldn't like it at all.

Him: Right, you wouldn't like it. Now, all our racial policies are trying to do is to support the very principles which you yourself believe in.

Me: I wouldn't want my daughter to marry a *white* man. I wouldn't want her to marry *any* man. She is only five years old. Is Dr. Jones advocating little girls getting married to old men? I think that's sick. That's disgusting. Where does he get that out of the Bible? I think that's—

Him: No, no. I meant that when she grows up, would you like her to marry a black man?

Me: Just the thought of it, my little, tiny daughter getting married. That's awful. Dr. Jones has some nerve calling me a Communist. I am going to condemn him from my pulpit next Sunday. It's a sin, a perversion! Little girls getting married before they even get a chance to be in kindergarten! It's an outrage!

Him: (Now shouting into the telephone)Would you listen to me! I am trying to tell you, if you'll just keep your mouth shut, that I was saying that, when your daughter got older, say twenty-five or so—

Me: Look, you stop talking about my daughter. You and Dr. Jones. Keep your hands off of her you dirty old—

Him: I can't believe that you are a minister of the Gospel. I can't believe that those people over at that church, even a *Methodist* church, put up with a preacher like you.

Me: You've got your nerve calling *me* a disgrace. At least I'm not advocating all sorts of sexual perversions like you and Dr. Jones.

Him: (Shouting even louder) I called to have a Christian-to-Christian discussion. Are you trying to make fun of me?

Me: No, I'm trying to keep from crying over you.

Him: That does it. I don't have to take this! (He slams down the receiver.)

Later the next week, on my way to work one morning, my car was hit in the rear by an older man who claimed that he was eating a banana and didn't see the light turn red. This seemed a reasonable explanation for why he crushed my bumper. We exchanged business cards. His card listed him as a professor of evangelism at Bob Jones University.

For the time being, I have sworn off having fun with the folk at Bob Jones. No more late-night phone calls for me. They play rough. Not that they scare me, but I have a wife and two children to think about. 🔑

THE HE**A**RT OF
RACISM

By Jean Caffey Lyles

From Issue #77/February–March, 1984

That first summer, when we drove to Texarkana to visit Jim's family for the first time, I donned my disguise in St. Louis for the drive through Arkansas—sunglasses, a curly black wig, and heavy theatrical makeup in a shade Max Factor called "dark umber."

It was 1971, and it wasn't safe for an inter-racial couple to be seen travelling together in a car through that part of the South. Or so we thought. If you didn't look too closely under the sunglasses, where the makeup ended around the eyes, and didn't hear the West Texas "Anglo" twang in my speech, the disguise was fairly convincing.

When we got to Texarkana, I took off the wig and scrubbed off the makeup. Whereupon Laura, my mother-in-law, said she thought I looked better in dark makeup, and why had I been in such a hurry to wash it off?

That first trip to Arkansas remains my one experience in "passing" as black. By the next summer, our fears of being a conspicuous target for the Klan or for some small-town southern sheriff had faded, and I remembered how uncomfortable it had been in the summer heat wearing a wig and the heavy, oil greasepaint.

98

I suspect that it wasn't only the heat that made the disguise uncomfortable. Wasn't there something dishonest about "playacting" at blackness when I was not willing to take on all the liabilities of *being* black? I could always wash off the greasepaint when we got to Laura's house. And wasn't there something cowardly about using the temporary protection of blackness to save me from the risks of the reality I had chosen—being inter-racially married in a society where black-white marriage was a taboo?

Was a taboo? *Is* a taboo!

In case I had forgotten, a reminder popped up recently on one of the TV morning shows. A writer of daytime soap operas was saying that she had been able to introduce story lines about teenage sex and drugs, homosexuality, and incest, without incurring the displeasure of the viewing audience. But there was one story line the viewers would simply not tolerate on their favorite soaps, and their objections were so vehement that the theme had to be dropped from the plot: inter-racial romance.

Forget the Gallup polls. That visceral reaction from ordinary daytime television watchers tells me more about the current American reality than any survey can.

Other institutions of white society may open up to blacks—the government, the Church, the corporation, the private club. But the white institution, the white family, is still off-limits.

Well, we knew that when we got married. Marriage is, like it or not, a political act, and marrying across racial lines always says a loud "NO" to that final, most sensitive cultural taboo. We discovered how strong the feelings are on this subject—which pervade the whole society—when we lost not only some white friends, but also some black friends.

White people who marry black people (or who adopt black children) are also making a theological statement. It's the same theological statement we learned at age four, in a Sunday School song: "Red and yellow, black and white, all are precious in His sight." And later, in adult Bible studies, "There is neither Jew nor Greek, there is neither slave nor free, there is neither male nor female, for you are all one in Christ Jesus."

But sooner or later, those of us who have married or adopted across racial lines learn that we can't kid ourselves and think that we have become honorary blacks and earned a lifetime exemption from dealing with the racism in our own heart and soul. Committing yourself to a black man or a black woman, or parenting a black child, may give you more sensitive antennae to detect racism in your friends, your relatives, your church, your community, your TV programs, or the whole culture. But I do not think that antennae necessarily pick up the signals of your own racism.

Bigotry lurks in all our hearts; no one is immune. (That, I think, is the lesson to be learned from Jesse Jackson's much-discussed remarks about Jewish New Yorkers. In a racist society, even blacks succumb to racism.)

You have not earned a permanent dispensation from dealing with your own racism, even if:

- You marched at Selma in the 60s.
- You don't laugh at ethnic jokes anymore.
- You purposely joined an integrated church and sent your kids to an integrated school.
- You know the difference between the "old racism" and the "new racism" and you think the "new" is not much of an improvement.
- You favor affirmative action and equal employment opportunity.
- You invited a black couple and a Filipino couple to your last dinner party.
- Your gynecologist is a Native American and your shrink is from the West Indies.
- You write eloquent editorials blasting your denomination's racist attitudes.
- You invited a black choir to sing at your church.
- You invited John Perkins, Bill Pannell, and Tom Skinner to speak at the big conference your group held last year.
- You really like the Japanese guy your sister married.
- You give money to the NAACP and the United Negro College Fund.
- You can sing all three verses of the black national anthem, "Lift Ev'ry Voice and Sing," by memory.
- You voted for Jesse Jackson.

Neither drowning in guilt nor giving ourselves little self-congratulatory pats on the back will heal us. Both the "old racism" and the "new racism" are alive and well, and each of us has to do what we can do. There are no exact prescriptions to keep them from finding permanent residence in our hearts. ▮

From Issue #62/August–September, 1981

Vexing Christa

The Maundy Thursday services at the Episcopal Cathedral of St. John the Divine in Manhattan included such now familiar symbols of a progressive liturgy as a dramatic reading and a symbolic dance. But when a four-foot bronze statue of Jesus on the cross was unveiled, gasps could be heard throughout the main chapel. The Christus was, in fact, a Christa, complete with undraped breasts and rounded hips.

The work, created in 1975 by Sculptor Edwina Sandys, 45, for the United Nations' Decade for Women, had been shown in galleries and art exhibits, but it had never before been displayed in a church. To New York Suffragan Bishop Walter Dennis, it was a "desecration" of Christian symbols. He urged parishioners to write the diocese's presiding bishop, the Rt. Rev. Paul Moore Jr., "if it shocks you as much as it did me." Cathedral Dean James Parks Morton, who organized the display with Moore's concurrence, responded that the effort to "send a positive message to women" had upset only the same people who oppose ordination for women. Said Sandys (who is the granddaughter of Winston Churchill): "It shows that the church still has power and that people do care."

As for those who made a point of walking behind the cathedral's main altar to have a look during the statue's ten-day showing, the reactions were mixed, but rarely mild. It was "not at all blasphemous" to Katherine Austin, who thought it reflected a mystic Christian view that "sees Christ as our mother." Beverly Stewart, on the other hand, said, "It's disgraceful. God and Christ are male. They're playing with a symbol we've believed in for all our lives." The Christa seemed to be doing her job as a focus for provocation, if not of prayer.

From Issue #78/April–May, 1984

A FEMININE FAITH

By Ben Patterson

From Issue #72/April–May, 1983

The best Mothers' Day sermon I ever heard had the provocative title, "Let's All Be Mothers." It had us all wondering, that title. Dr. Vernard Eller, the man who preached the sermon, assured us early on that what he had in mind was not that we all be mothers in the biological sense, but that we take all of the so-called motherly qualities—self-sacrifice, unselfishness, and compassion—and see them not as virtues restricted to mothers only, but as Christian virtues that apply equally to both sexes, regardless of parental status.

Of course. It is a diabolical perversion of the meaning of motherhood that would take all of its best qualities and restrict them only to one sex, and then to only a subdivision of that sex—mothers. That is sexism with a new twist! Let us all be sacrificial and unselfish in our love; let us all be mothers.

That sermon set me to thinking of another, related issue. Why are there more women in the church than men? No one seems to have absolutely reliable statistics, but the indicators appear to be something like a ratio of 60 percent to 40 percent, female to male, in most Christian congregations. The figures Christian booksellers use in their marketing strategies are even more disproportionate. They point to a reading public that is about 80 percent female.

Why is that so? The reasons are probably varied and complex, but I want to suggest one: the fact that many Christian virtues are perceived by our culture as feminine. The perception is correct. God is revealed in Scripture as masculine. He is King; we are His subjects. He is father; we are His children. But supremely, He is revealed as the husband to us—His wife. He positions Himself toward us as leader, initiator and ruler—all masculine qualities. What that in turn calls forth from us is to follow, respond, and submit—all feminine qualities.

I don't want to argue here whether these descriptions of masculinity and femininity are purely human cultural concoctions, or built into the very structure of human existence by God Himself. I happen to believe the latter is indeed the case. But, for the sake of argument, let us leave that question alone and affirm what seems to be undeniable—that in our culture the masculine has been perceived, at least, and continues to be perceived, in terms of leader, initiator, and ruler. Likewise, the feminine has been perceived in terms of follower and submitter.

This being the case, males in our culture have been accurate in their perception that Christianity is biased toward the feminine, for it calls us to be feminine in our response to God's masculine; to be wife to His husband, child to His father, and subject to His King.

Am I proposing that it is easier for women in our culture to be Christians than it is for men? Yes, I am. For whatever reasons, women are more predisposed to open themselves and to be receptive and sensitive to the Word of God. They are still sinners, no less and no more than their male counterparts. But just as in the history of Christian missions, some peoples have proven to be more ripe for the Gospel than others, so there are components to female identity that make them more receptive than males to God's Word.

Many Christian virtues are perceived by our culture as feminine.

The paradigm for this is the Virgin Mary's response to the angel Gabriel's announcement that she was to be made with child by the Holy Spirit. Her response was, "I am the Lord's servant. May it be to me as you have said." She can only receive and submit. Karl Barth comments eloquently on this event when he writes, ". . . from the human standpoint, the male is excluded here. The male has nothing to do with this birth. What is included here is, if you like, a divine act of judgment. To what is to begin here, man is to contribute nothing by his action and his initiative . . . the male, as the specific agent of human action and history, with his responsibility for directing the human species, must now retire into the background, as the powerless figure of Joseph." (*Dogmatics in Outline*, p. 99).

Highlighting this even more is the sharp contrast provided by the reaction of Zechariah to the announcement of the miraculous birth of John the Baptist. He tells Gabriel that he and his wife are old. How can he be sure this birth will happen? Mary too wants to know how, but not as Zechariah does. Where she wants to know how *God* can do it, he wants to know how *he* can do it. He is typically male in his response to God. He must be the initiator and the manager, and if he cannot, how can this thing take place? Gabriel lets Zechariah know, in no uncertain terms, exactly how God feels about that kind of presumption and defiance. He is struck dumb until John is born. Mary, on the other hand, sings the Magnificat.

Mary is venerated by the Roman Catholics, and for good reason. Despite the excesses of Mariology, or Mariolatry if you will, the message of Mary holds true. She, not Zechariah or Joseph, is the model of what it means to stand in a proper relationship to God. The conception of her child Jesus is not a sexual event, it is a faith event. Early Christian art portrayed this by depicting the entry of the Holy Spirit into Mary's body as through her ear, not her sexual organs. She hears and receives the Word of God.

The feminist movement has impacted the Church in many ways, some good and some bad. It has correctly put before us the rightful place women should occupy in the leadership of the Church, on all levels and in all areas. It has not been helpful, however, when it has told women that the way to achieve that rightful status is by becoming more like their male adversaries. The old dictum that the conquerors always take on the traits of the vanquished is never more true than it is here, and with a vengeance. Feminism will have much more to offer the Church if it can teach women to lead as women, not as men, and crucial—to teach men to become better Christians by learning to be more feminine.

Men must learn to be feminine in their response to God. They must be taught the virtues of silence and receptivity, submission, and obedience. They must learn not to hide from themselves their weakness and dependence, but to let these things become the point of contact with their King and father and husband God.

Likewise, men must learn to be more feminine toward one another. In the church I pastor, the most significant thing happening spiritually is happening among our women. They readily reach out to each other to nurture and to care, to bear one another's burdens and to

> # Men must learn to be feminine in their response to God.

listen and respond to the needs of their sisters. When our men gather together, there is always a lot of fun and laughter, but beyond that not much. We slap each others' backs, punch each other in the arm and generally avoid letting each other know who we are and where we hurt. With all of the loud camaraderie, there is the poignancy of men who need each other but who are not sure how to connect.

Our sisters could teach us how. We could learn to be more feminine without becoming any less masculine. More important, we would learn to be more Christian. We would learn that power and authority are demonic without gentleness, and that the solitary, self-sufficient male is given the same evaluation by God now as he was given in the Garden—not good. He needs a partner; he needs a woman. Paradoxically, he needs to learn from her that he can become more himself by becoming more like her.

From Issue #51/October– November, 1979

MACHO
FEMINISM

By Jean Caffey Lyles
From Issue #72/April–May, 1983

At a conference on "Speaking the Truth to Power" at New York's Riverside Church, the Reverend William Sloan Coffin once ventured the opinion that "the women's liberation that is most needed is the liberation of the woman in every man." He was almost immediately zapped by feminist theologian Rosemary Ruether, who objected that what Coffin and other men who make such statements are doing is co-opting the liberation of women into the liberation of men.

"This suppressed side of them," said Ruether, "is *not* 'the woman in them.' As long as we perpetuate that language, we perpetuate a confusion." She went on to say that this "ultimate co-optation of women" is most frequently practiced by clergy and psychologists. "It makes them feel good. It gives them the illusion that they are feminist."

Not only do men want to have the illusion that they are feminist—they want *us* to have that illusion. It's getting harder and harder to tell the man who is *really* a feminist from the one who's putting on a pretty good act.

There is, to be sure, a certain absence of subtlety in this method of turning the women's movement into the men's movement. A more sophisticated approach is the one employed by my friend Fred, the Christian feminist.

Let me tell you about Fred. He is

the most sensitive, open, vulnerable, caring person you ever met, and when you share a problem with him (in Fred's crowd, you don't just "tell" something, you "share" it), he will give you his warm, tender, understanding look and say, "I can resonate with that."

He talks a lot about "parenting" and how there is really no difference between what male parents and female parents ought to do for their kids. He tells you he spends more time with the kids than his spouse does. (Fred always calls Edie his "spouse" instead of his "wife," a word that has come to sound to him a little sexist.)

He will tell you about "our" experience having the last baby by the Lamaze method. Fred took a six-month paternity leave afterward, of course, and he always got up for the 2 a.m. feeding. All of Fred and Edie's kids have names like "Terry" and "Lee" and "Leslie" and "Chris," so you're not sure whether they're boys or girls when you first hear the names. Fred says it would be sexist to just give the girls girls' names and the boys boys' names.

Fred is inordinately proud of his dishpan hands, every patch of red, roughened skin. He earned them honestly, standing many evenings at the kitchen sink, up to his elbows in dishwater.

Fred makes sure you know that he's the one who gets up and makes coffee for the household in the morning. He and Edie share the cooking and housework 50/50. He never says, "I'm helping Edie" or "I'm babysitting," which would imply that the tasks at hand weren't really his job.

When Mrs. Goodbody from the church called up to ask Edie to make four dozen cookies for the youth fellowship, Fred got a little miffed. Why did they always ask Edie to bake cookies and never him? He really bakes better cookies—Edie is into pies.

If Fred comes to your house for dinner, he is the one who will get up from the table to help you clear the dishes before the dessert course—and he'll do it before it occurs to any of the women to volunteer.

At his office, Fred never slips and calls the secretaries "girls" or "gals" instead of "women." And he will correct anyone who commits such an error. Very gently, of course.

He is always careful to say "chairperson" and "clergyperson" and "congressperson" and "craftsperson" and even "freshperson." His language is impeccable when he asks, "Does everyone have his or her ticket?" (To be scrupulously fair, next time he will say "her or his.") In writing, he uses "his/her," "her/his," and "she/he."

Fred does not wait for women to get out of the elevator first. He believes that whoever is standing in the front of the elevator should go ahead and exit. He will not offer to help you on with your coat unless you really need help—and then he will do it whether you're male or female. He believes whoever gets there first should open the door—or whoever's carrying the smallest load.

He tells you how much he admires strong women—and how he is much too secure about his own sexuality to feel threatened by a woman who is forceful and assertive.

In fact, Fred is so secure about his sexuality that he is not embarrassed for people to know that he does needlework. He sits right there in Administrative Council meeting and works on his latest stitchery project, a suitable-for-framing motto for his daughter that says, "Girls Can Be Anything."

Fred's wife, Edie, just got a promotion to a job that is considered "executive-level." Fred is being very supportive about the fact that she may be staying later at the office some evenings. He made a point of telling two of his colleagues, with some pride, that Edie is now making more money than he is.

Fred believes that it is OK for men to cry—and women too, if they want to—and he's not ashamed to tell you that he cried most of the way through *E.T.*

Well, as you can see, on a scale of 1 to 10, from total chauvinism to perfect feminism, Fred is an 11-1/2. Fred is a better feminist than I am, or than I will ever be. And like all absolutely perfect feminists, or absolutely perfect anything-elses, he is also something of a pain.

Nobody can beat Fred at feminism—not even Letha Scanzoni or Virginia Ramey Mollenkott. If there is a "More-Feminist-Than-Thou" trophy, Fred has already won it.

What this gentle, sensitive, nurturing man has done—it finally dawns on me—is to turn feminism into a contest: a highly competitive, aggressive, individual sport, one at which he competes brilliantly and relentlessly and always wins.

It's a little disillusioning to discover just how macho feminism can be.

Truth Is Stranger Than Fiction

WOMEN PROBLEMS ? ?

Having difficulties with women in your church? Our 126 page paperback with approx. 200 scriptures should help. It's serious, funny, and very candid ! ! $3.00 covers all.

MARGIN NOTES

A black sheep has a much sharper sense of smell than a white sheep.

It has been proven that more men than women cry at the movies.

Women tend to be more satisfied with their first name than men.

Sitting Bull's original name as a youth was Jumping Badger.

The female dog is more likely to bite than the male.

6

The Strands of Hair That You Comb Over to Cover Your Bald Spot

Image-Making

Baldness is nothing to be ashamed of; in fact, it has some distinct advantages:

It's spiritual. My theory is that a bald person's hair has simply been raptured early. (By rapturing early, you miss rush-hour traffic.)

It's poetic. Baldness has inspired such moving lines as . . . "He's not bald. He just has a tall face." Or . . . "From a short distance away, it looks like his neck is blowing bubble gum." Or . . . "Barbers don't charge him for cutting his hair. They charge him for searching for it."

It's practical. When you're bald, you don't have to worry about hairstyles; as far as I know, you don't even have to worry about scalp styles. Hairy people, on the other hand, have to spend an incredible amount of time grooming. For example, I read the true account of a woman in Britain who has hair seventy-six inches long. She uses an entire container of shampoo each time she washes her hair, and she has to stretch her hair out the length of the bathtub to do the washing.

Most bald people can pass the same container of shampoo down through four generations of bald relatives, making it a family heirloom.

Because baldness is so wonderfully practical, it

amazes me that some people try to cover bald spots with those little strings of side hair. Not only is this unnecessary; it's futile. Trying to cover your bald spot with a string of hair is like trying to cover the Sahara Desert with a Speedo swimsuit.

Such attempts to disguise baldness make me think of certain churches that go to similarly futile lengths to improve their image by focusing on huge membership rolls and big bank accounts. The baldness of their faith always shows through.

The Door has a long history of uncovering churches obsessed with the big and the beautiful, including the church with the world's largest Sunday school, where their membership motto is, "If you're within 100 yards of us or our bus, you count."

Image-making at its silliest. That's what this chapter is all about. 🔑

Truth Is Stranger Than Fiction

From Issue #82/December, 1984–January, 1985

AEROBICS
M W F 9:00 AM
M THUR 7 PM
WORSHIP 10 AM

As a special Wittenburg Door exclusive, we print here excerpts from an interview with noted Church Death expert, Dr. Toulouse LaJaw. Dr. LaJaw escorted us into his spacious office, which overlooks beautiful downtown Newark. On the wall behind his large and cluttered desk was the inspiring symbol of the Church Death movement: the descending dove crashing into a barren fig tree. True to his reputation for flamboyance, Dr. LaJaw would frequently change the subject or ignore our questions, while doing an embarrassingly poor imitation of an energetic go-go dancer on his desk.

CHURCH DEATH AMERICA

By William D. Eisenhower
From Issue #63/December, 1981–
January, 1982

Door: Dr. LaJaw, um . . . could you please sit down for a minute?

LaJaw: My world is empty without you, babe.

Door: Er . . . Well, Dr. LaJaw, if it wouldn't be too much trouble, we were wondering if you—?

LaJaw: Hmmm?

Door: Yes, thank you for letting go of your ceiling fan. Now then, we appreciate it very much that you have interrupted your busy schedule to talk to us. We would like to begin by asking you to characterize the present state of the church.

LaJaw: Well, well, well, WELL! Am I glad you asked me *THAT*! The Church has made tremendous strides during the last decade or so. Why, I remember back in a more turbulent time, March of '68, I think it was, I was visiting my grandmother's church in New York City one Sunday, when right in the middle of the pastoral prayer several men stormed into the sanctuary and pushed the pastor right out of the pulpit! They all had machine guns, black jackets, black sunglasses, and combat boots. As one of them began speaking into the pulpit microphone, my grandmother cried out, "Good Heavens! Is it Youth Sunday *AGAIN*?" I tried to be reassuring, but of course, I had to admit that I wasn't sure. Then I heard another of the men angrily demanding reparations for the sins which the church had committed during the past year, and I realized what was going on. After all, this was a Methodist church. So, I turned back to my grandmother and said, "No, it's not Youth Sunday. I think that's the Administrative Board, and this is

Stewardship Sunday."

(At this point, Dr. LaJaw leaped out of his office and began running up and down the hall, laughing uncontrollably. An hour and forty-five minutes later, we got him to settle down, hoping that the interview might be resumed. But instead, Dr. LaJaw directed a question at us.)

Dr. LaJaw: Do you believe in myths?

Door: Um, do you mean . . . uh, like the disclosive power which resides in the language of ancient mythology and which often expresses itself in the dreams of people today? Yes, I'd say that we believe in myths as manifestations of the unconscious. Is that what you mean?

Dr. LaJaw: No, no, no, *NO*! I mean, do you believe in stupid, old stories about the gods that aren't true!?!

Door: But that's ridiculous! Dr. LaJaw, we came here to talk to you about the Church Death movement.

Dr. LaJaw: Oh—the *CHURCH DEATH* movement.

Door: That's right.

Dr. LaJaw: The movement of Church Death.

Door: Yes, that's right.

Dr. LaJaw: I see.

Door: Would it be asking too much for you to tell us something about it?

Dr. LaJaw: Not at all, not at all, *NOT AT ALL*! We here at the Church Death Institute have a story to tell. We have a mission. Church Death is a serious business and every minute counts. There is no point in wasting any—

Door: Well, then perhaps we could help move things along a little bit by asking you what the Church Death movement is all about.

Dr. LaJaw: *THAT'S* an easy one. Everyone knows that it is the big churches which are the important ones. I made that point very clear in my very first book, *Your Church is Too Small*. By now I think everyone generally agrees with me that it is the large congregations which really count.

Door: Well, but now—

Dr. LaJaw: Our ministry here at the Church Death Institute is very simply a work undertaken in obedience to the Word, and empowered by the Spirit—to the end that we help clear away the many, many, many, MANY smaller churches which have been cluttering up America over the years. Everybody knows that if a church isn't growing, it's worthless. Dinky churches don't glorify God. God is big and our churches need to be big, too. But before we began our ministry, there were thousands of churches out there that were just too puny to witness to the mighty things that God can do. So—the service which we render consists largely in putting these smaller churches out of their misery.

Door: I see. A sort of ecclesiastical euthanasia.

Dr. LaJaw: Yes, yes. Christians need to belong to the important churches, the successful churches—the churches where the Word is preached with power, and the senior pastor makes $55,000 or so. And it is our sincere hope that once all the useless churches have been erased from the American landscape, Christians will all have to become Possibility Thinkers by default.

Door: You mean . . . they'll all join the bigger churches once their's are gone?

Dr. LaJaw: Exactly! It's all so simple, isn't it? And think of what a powerful witness we are creating: nothing on the American horizon but gigantic steeples seated on top of vigorous, booming churches. What an *IMPACT* Christianity is starting to have!

Door: OK, we are with you so far, Dr. LaJaw. But now the crucial question is how small are the small churches which your organization ministers to?

Dr. LaJaw: Well, yes, that is the crucial question: How small is too small? There has been quite a lot of debate within the Church Death community about that. My own position is that the Bible is quite plain about where the cut-off point is supposed to be.

Door: Um . . . and . . . where is the cut-off point?

Dr. LaJaw: Six hundred and sixty-six. Any church with that many members or less is obviously too small to be doing anybody any good.

Door: Wait a minute! You're saying that a church with 666 members is too small?

Dr. LaJaw: Yes, that's right. Too small, or to use a technical designation currently in use by Church Death scholars, any congregation with 666 or less is what we like to refer to as a "worthless piece of trash."

Door: But that's an awfully high cut-off point, isn't it?

Dr. LaJaw: Perhaps it is, but it's a number I got out of the Bible, and you can't argue with Scripture.

Door: You can if you're a Presbyterian.

Dr. LaJaw: Good God! You're not Presbyterians, are you?

Door: How could we be Presbyterians? Do we look like All-American football players to you?

Dr. LaJaw: Hmm . . . I guess not.

Door: That's better. But now the one thing you haven't told us is exactly how it is that you go about ministering to these churches which you consider too small.

Dr. LaJaw: Well, of course, any church

above 666 we refer to our sister organization, the Church *GROWTH* Institute. The smaller ones we minister to with our own procedures.

Door: And what does that entail?

Dr. LaJaw: Firebombing, mostly. That, and we put on some regional workshops, too.

Door: Wait a minute! You mean you actually go out and blow up buildings and burn down sanctuaries?

Dr. LaJaw: No, no, no, *NO!* That would be horrible.

Door: I should say so!

Dr. LaJaw: No, what we usually do is contract that service out to one of our subsidiary firms. We have several that we are allied with. The largest is called The Incendiary Fellowship, but there are several others. Since Church Death is an issue with cross-cultural significance, we have planted some sister firms among the ethnic minorities. We have a ministry group which does our firebombings in East Los Angeles which is called Los Tamales Calientes, and another one opening pretty soon up in San Francisco's Chinatown, called Tongs of Fire.

At this point, Dr. Toulouse LaJaw broke into the opening lines of "Take the Last Train to Clarksville" and bolted for a table in the corner. We stood up and bid him a fond farewell. On our way out of his office, we looked again at the emblem on LaJaw's wall, and agreed it was a beautifully universal symbol which could easily serve to represent most of the organizations currently ministering to the Church.

HOW TO SPEND
$15,000,000.00

By Wayne Rice

From Issue #44/August–September, 1978

You can spend it this way:

Build and make operational 100 food canneries in poor countries, which would preserve seasonal crops, providing a constant food supply, livelihood and dignity for approximately 400,000 families.	$1,500,000
Support 10 orphanages in Nairobi for the next five years, providing food and shelter for over 1,000 children.	180,000
Feed 11,000 children presently suffering from malnutrition in the West Indies every day for at least the next five years. (The money could be used to buy the food and build a warehouse capable of storing it without spoilage.)	140,000
Provide interest-free loan money that would allow 300 poor families in the rural south to build a home and start a small farm or business. (The money would be paid back and used again in a few years.)	1,000,000
Completely renovate a 45-room building in downtown Washington D.C. to provide emergency shelter for evicted families and the homeless during the winter months.	80,000
Provide a full year of clinical care for 1,000 critically ill children in Bangladesh.	1,250,000
Build new housing for 1,000 families and rebuild 20 churches and schools destroyed by cyclones in India.	1,140,000
Supply a medical clinic in southern Sudan, Africa, with needed drugs and medications to save the lives of diseased children for the next 20 years. (Presently, 30 percent of all children there die before age five.)	150,000
Dig and install 50 water wells in Gujarat, India, where people suffer severe poverty and malnutrition because of lack of irrigation for farming.	410,000
Start a university in Azua, southwest Dominican Republic. The university would educate and train 500 full-time students in agriculture, mechanics, teaching, and medicine in an area with an 80-percent unemployment rate. (You could also provide loan money for the tuition of the first 500 students.)	150,000

114

Establish a chain of 20 co-op grocery stores in economically depressed U.S. communities to make quality food available at reasonable prices to low-income families. The money would also keep the stores operating for the next 10 years.	140,000
Hire five top marketing experts who would find and implement ways to sell the products of Third World countries, providing an economic base for literally thousands of people.	500,000
Establish 100 new schools in Haiti and operate them for the next 10 years—providing an education for 10,000 children in a country with only a 19 percent literacy rate.	2,400,000
Send 1,000 underprivileged young people to a week of camp at the Forest Home Christian Conference Center.	75,000
Open and supply 10 kitchens and free clinics to provide care and nourishment for the poor and homeless in 10 major cities in the United States.	250,000
Send two teams of Wycliffe missionaries to a previously unreached South American tribe (5,000 people) for 15 years to learn the language, translate Scripture and publish 5,000 New Testaments.	470,000
Put 50 ministerial students through the most expensive evangelical seminary in the world (Fuller) to receive an M. Div. degree, and support them for five years so they can begin new churches wherever they choose.	3,220,000
Build a seminary in Africa. Then staff and operate it for the next 10 years.	1,325,000
Build ten orphanages, which would house 750 to 1,000 children over the age of six—children who would have otherwise become slaves. (In Caphaitian, Haiti, one out of five children are orphans and most are acquired by wealthier families as bond servants.)	100,000
Print 200,000 Bibles for free distribution to every person presently incarcerated in state and federal penitentiaries.	380,000
Build 70 new homes in Tijuana, Mexico, to provide shelter for families left homeless following flooding.	140,000
TOTAL COST	$15,000,000

Or you can spend it this way:

Build a big glass church.	$15,000,000
TOTAL COST	$15,000,000

This feature first appeared in 1978, so figures are based on prices then. The figures were all documented, and most represented urgent needs that lacked only the funding for implementation. Sources: World Vision, Wycliffe Bible translators, Dr. Anthony Campolo, Kefa Sempangi, Fuller Seminary, Koinonia Farms, Forest Home, Larry Holbert (Catholic Worker House), American Bible Society, Voice of Calvary Ministries.

EVANGELICAL GIGOLO

By Mike Yaconelli
From Issue #55/June–July, 1980

He stood in front of the television camera, his eyes ablaze with conviction, his voice charged with emotion. With every hair in place and not a wrinkle in his three-piece, baby-blue suit, Jim Bakker shouted to anyone who was listening, "We are not losers, we're winners!" I turned my television off and sat quietly in the room, disturbed by an unknown source of anxiety. It wasn't until a few days later that I discovered what was bothering me. What frightened me then, and what frightens me now, is the sin of power.

I believe that evangelicals have sold their birthright for a mess of porridge. We have been seduced by the glitter and temporariness of power and have gone a whoring. We have sold out and traded our worship of God for the worship of power. We have exchanged the ministry of sacrifice for the ministry of domination. We have decided to be strong instead of weak, the majority instead of the minority, the conqueror instead of the conquered, the winner instead of the loser.

The Church has been mesmerized by power. We stand in awe of the beauty queen, the pro football player, the wealthy businessman; and we willingly pay millions of dollars to anyone who will take our money and prove to us that we are the majority. That we are respectable. That we are winners.

We gladly allow these personages of power to travel in their private jets with their loyal platoon of executive assistants and press secretaries. We gladly give our substance to vicariously share with them as they wine and dine with presidents, scurry from one TV studio to the next, and whisk in and out of airports in long, black limousines. These power personalities have become our evangelical gigolos. We gladly prostitute our money, our time and all that we have, so that we can flaunt them in front of those who do not believe that we are, in fact, winners. And it isn't their fault. It is ours.

We need these heroes. We want, in the worst way, to believe that we are right. That we are going to win. That we are going to be the conquerors. Instead of faith, we ask for success. Instead of discipleship, we want entertainment. Instead of changed lives, we are more satisfied with high standings on the latest Gallup poll.

Jacques Ellul put it this way: "In the world, everyone wants to be a wolf, and no one is called to play the part of the sheep. Yet the world cannot live without this living witness of sacrifice. That is why it is essential

116

that Christians should be very careful not to be wolves in the spiritual sense; that is, people who dominate others. Christians must accept the domination of other people and offer the daily sacrifice of their lives, which is united with the sacrifice of Jesus Christ."

When will we understand that we have been seduced by the evil one and are no longer wrestling against principalities and powers, but have joined with them to try and dominate our culture? We may be considered winners, but it is God who loses.

"Well, Higgins, looks like the Building Committee targeted the right people during their fund raiser."

From Issue #108/November–December, 1989

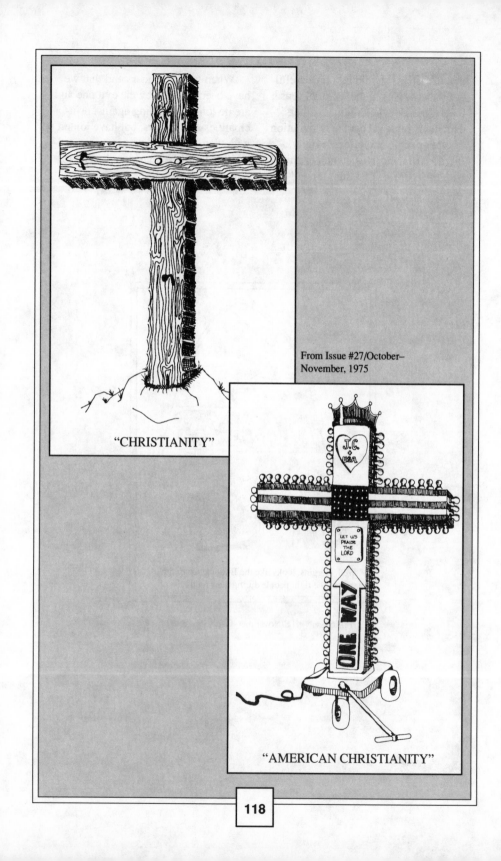

From Issue #27/October–November, 1975

"CHRISTIANITY"

"AMERICAN CHRISTIANITY"

The Host Church

Bethel Church of San Jose, host of the annual Singing Christmas Tree, was privileged to move into its new facility during 1980, located at 1201 So. Winchester Blvd.

The photographs on this page give a glimpse of its beauty; the following statistics are certainly of interest:

- 7.5 Acres
- 83,000 sq. ft. (2 acres under roof)
- 4,089 ft. of pews
- 10,000 sq. ft. of carpeting
- 300 tons of air conditioning
- 50,000 sq. ft. of tile on roof
- Almost 1 million board feet of lumber
- 32-channel sound system

Dedicated to the Glory of God October 5, 1980

From Issue #58/December, 1980–January, 1981

Truth Is Stranger Than Fiction

THE WOMAN'S GUILD OF SAINT PETER'S EPISCOPAL CHURCH
110 North Warson Road
Invites you to attend
THE 1986 LENTEN CHRISTIAN EDUCATION SERIES

TUESDAY, JANUARY 21, 1986, 1:00 – 3:00 P.M.
"A FASHION SEMINAR FOR WOMEN"
Jan McCormick

Jan McCormick currently models for Neiman Marcus and has free lanced in her profession for 20 years, as well as coordinated fashion shows and seminars for 15 years. She is an entertaining, informative speaker who helps make fashion and dressing fun — not a chore.

TUESDAY, JANUARY 28, 1986, 1:00 – 3:00 P.M.
"ORIENTAL RUGS AND TODAY'S WORLD MARKET"
Usef Hakimian

Mr. Usef Hakimian is the chief executive officer of Hakimian International Industries in New York and the president of Hakimian Industries in Saint Louis. The Hakimian Company maintains departments with the May Company in Saint Louis, Denver, and Cleveland and with all of the Bloomingdale stores. An oriental rug will give its owner a lifetime of service, pride in ownership and will add opulence to any home decor. The oriental rug business has changed drastically in the past 20 years. Mr. Hakimian will discuss what is happening in today's market.

TUESDAY, FEBRUARY 4, 1986, 1:00 – 3:00 P.M.
"APPRAISALS OF YOUR VALUABLES"
Bruce Selkirk, Jr.

Bruce Selkirk from Selkirk Galleries of Saint Louis will evaluate and appraise one (1) item per person. You may bring any porcelain, silver, china, crystal, carpet, or furniture piece to be appraised. Mr. Selkirk cannot appraise any rare books, manuscripts, coins, stamps, prints, Japanese or Chinese art, or any framed art.

TUESDAY, FEBRUARY 11, 1986, 1:00 – 3:00 P.M.
"PICTURE FRAMING"
Sandy Miller

Mrs. Sandy Miller, manager of the Clayton Frame Factory, will give a step-by-step demonstration of all the framing techniques their shop offers. She will be happy to answer any and all of your questions and urges you to bring a print, oil, or piece of needlework from home that she can help you with.

TUESDAY, FEBRUARY 18, 1986, 1:00 – 3:00 P.M.
"DO'S AND DON'TS OF REAL ESTATE"
MaDonna Lee

MaDonna Lee is a lifetime member of the Missouri Real Estate Association and is presently associated with Caldwell-Banker/Ira E. Berry in their Ladue office. She has been selling real estate for over 15 years in Saint Louis and is considered a real pro in her field. She will be speaking on all aspects of buying or selling a house.

From Issue #89/February–March, 1989

From Issue #71/February–March, 1983

MINISTRY

A MAGAZINE FOR CLERGY

JULY 1980

Your tie, more than any other apsect of your appearance, will determine how people view your credibility, personality, and ability. Conservative patterns symbolize respectability and responsibility.

The most acceptable dress shirts are white. Greater moral strengths are attributed to those who wear white shirts than to those who wear shirts of other colors. Pale, solid colors are acceptable substitutes for white, with pale blue being the most popular. Pink and lavender are too feminizing, and a man should never wear a solid red shirt, no matter who he is or what he does!

CLOTHING MEN OF THE CLOTH

A trait common to all successful executives is that they always have their hair combed.

When properly tied, the tip of the tie should come just to the belt buckle. Bow ties give a negative impression.

Asked to select the men who were the most sympathetic, effective, well-educated ministers, the majority chose individuals in a conservatively cut, dark, two-piece suit. The pin-striped, three-piece business suit was rejected as often as was the leisure suit.

A minister wearing a conservatively cut, dark, two-piece suit is judged as sympathetic, effective, and well-educated.

A well-dressed minister keeps his shoes shined.

From Issue #56/August–September, 1980

From Issue #30/April–May, 1976

JEREMIAH OF JERUSALEM

Mr. Jesus Bar Joseph
Joseph and Sons Carpentry
Nazareth, Judea 20213

Dear Jesus,

Word has reached the city of your activities and aspirations. We are impressed and would like to suggest that it is time for you to consider employing a public relations firm to represent you.

Should you choose Jeremiah of Jerusalem, here are some of the things we can do for you . . .

1.   We can do a complete analysis of your background and qualifications so that a personality profile can be developed. Such things as the rumors of your illegitimate birth, family background in Nazareth and your friendship with publicans and sinners will need to be played down, of course.

2.   We can improve the image of your disciples. Some of them, as you know, have pretty seedy reputations. Our publicity department can do wonders with drawings that reduce the offense of long hair and beards. We could also suggest a couple of outstanding young men to replace the tax collector and the political radical zealot.

3.   We can prepare your press releases so that all the political and religious factions hear what they want to hear. You can't be too careful in this regard and you obviously could use our expertise.

4.   We can suggest other publicity stunts like the healings and miracles that you have already pulled off. That feeding of the multitude was a winner, but more follow-up was needed. How about jumping off the temple during a feast day or a grand entry into Jerusalem with a Roman legion escort, the temple marching band, and network press coverage?

5. We can improve your relationships with those in high places. We have contacts with the religious and government biggies. Both Pilate and Herod are in our hip pocket. I'm afraid you've made some real blunders in this area, but we can fix things up, I'm sure.

6. We can establish offices for you in the heart of Jerusalem. Our understanding is that you have no headquarters and are difficult to reach as you roam around the countryside mingling with the commoners. This is no way to operate a successful Messiahship program.

I'm sure the need for our services has become obvious and we will be delighted to make a complete proposal. You'll find our commission percentage rate quite competitive. We have represented the best of Messianic hopefuls and we know you will find our experience unsurpassed. (John the Baptist turned down our help, and you know what happened to him!)

Yours for better P.R.,

Jeremiah

JEREMIAH OF JERUSALEM

P.S.—A logo is needed for instant recognition that can be put on chariot bumpers, T-Togas, and jewelry. I have an idea you may like. How about this: ⊂IΧΘΥΣ✕ I designed it for a fish merchant who didn't buy it. If you'll notice, the first two letters are the first two letters of Jesus-Messiah in Greek. We could work something up for the rest, I'm sure.

JJ:jm

> **By Dave A. Sheffel**
>
> From Issue #27/October–November, 1975

CORINTH FIRST CHURCH

Corinth, Greece—Rev. T. Carswell Maximus

TO: *Paul, Apostle*
FROM: *Corinth First Church*
    Corinth, Greece

Dear Paul,

Well, my friend, a few days after we got your two letters, we had a board meeting at Corinth First Church. Let me tell you, it was a rough go-around.

Your letters caused no little stir here, believe me. Like, we're talking heavy, Paul. Most of us—Brother Earnest and Sister Emily Grandbucks included—feel that you're being a little too rough on us.

Standards are fine, Paul, but let's face it: we're all living in this town together, and we have to get along. Bending the rules a little seems the prudent thing to do. Besides, you know who, though he may be living (so you say) in "sin," does tithe. And our treasury would sorely miss him. Besides which, it's a personal family matter—and we feel the church here in Corinth has no real right to butt into personal matters. After all, what our members do on their own time is their own business, wouldn't you agree?

Regarding the funds you asked us to send you—the Disbursement Committee (having no other time to do so) meets Wednesday night in our new Grandbucks Fellowship Hall during service. Consequently, this extremely important group of our members missed the general membership vote on your fund request; and, not having their essential input, well, we had to table the issue, thereby keeping the funds in 11-percent C.D.'s for another year. You'll agree, I'm sure, that this is great for the building fund.

Here's the good news. We have our eye on a piece of property across town that we think we can get down-zoned since one of our members is on the Corinth City Council. And, dear brother, Grandbucks is on the Corinth National Bank's board—so the financing will be no problem.

I'm quite enthusiastic about our building program, dear Paul. We're up to three services on Sunday mornings, and we hope to exceed 10,000 in attendance on Easter. Incidentally, we have four elders set to dress up like giant bunnies and hide gaily colored eggs in the choir loft for the kids. How God blesses.

As to your plea for "walking around" money—please forgive me, but are you truly being an effective steward? Watching those pennies? Perhaps you could follow our lead and have a garage sale. We made more than $126 last month with one, and it kept 375 of us busy, busy, busy—for the Lord, of course. I must say, Paul, I disagree entirely with your admonition to avoid using the courts. We have initiated a lawsuit against First Church of Laodicia for the recovery of a certain letter which we know they have and which they say they've misplaced. In your letter, your warning to avoid lawsuits—well it's reasonable to assume that civilized people would behave in a civilized way . . . Hence, we must disregard your warning and hope the courts will straighten out this tiff we're *having within the brotherhood. Good common sense has always proven effective in matters such as these.*

Our "bus ministry" is going fine. We have come up with the idea of hiding little packs of bubble gum under the bus seats. The kids get on the bus for the bubble gum, then—zap! We close the doors and "spirit" them off to church. We're calling it our "Kapture the Kids for Khrist" program. We have 238 kids at each Sunday service now. I must admit, though, with all of them blowing bubbles, it gets rather hectic at times.

Speaking of hectic, your friend, Timothy, whom you sent to us, is causing problems. Frankly, it seems he's a bit of a fanatic. Now Paul, we both know that too much of a good thing can be too much, if you get my drift. Nough said.

As to your proposed wintertime visit—sure, we look forward to seeing you but, next time, please give us a little more warning when you plan on dropping in. Since we're in the midst of a building program, we really don't have the time for any lengthy speeches. Our motto: Let's get the job done and get it done now!

Well, old and trusted friend, I'll close now. And please, take my advice and go to a qualified ophthalmologist about the problem you're always complaining about.

Yours, and trusting entirely in Him,
I remain,

By Robert J. Hensler

From Issue #88/December, 1985–January, 1986

Reverend Doctor T. Carswell Maximus
D.D., Ph.D., L.L.B.A.

The New Pastoral Robe committee reports a slight mix-up in the shipment received.

Well, let's not be too hasty, fellas.

From Issue #108/November–December, 1989

Linda Emery Ministries

Dear Friends:

As you know, the economy in general, and Linda Emery Ministries specifically, have recently fallen on hard times. Undaunted by financial disaster, our dream of finding that one special soul was still alive but floundering.

In fact, we were on the brink of despair until one day last week when, after doing extensive, first-hand research on the evils of drinking, I looked out the window and beheld a 32-foot-high chipmunk. I immediately recognized this as a sign from God because no one else who was there could see it.

As I stood there in awe, the chipmunk told me to covenant with our constituents in an act of faith concerning the construction of a baptismal found that far exceeded any dreams we might have had.

The dimensions would be 20' by 30' (in an irregular design resembling a kidney bean) with steps at one end and a board at the other for convenient entry. Dressing rooms and shower stalls would be located in the flower garden on the north side of the found. On the south side, a small building, completely furbished in cedar, would be used for prebaptismal meditation. A high-intensity heater would be installed in this building for the specific purpose of symbolizing to the subject his passage from hell to heaven as he dashes from this room to the refreshing, moderately heated found.

We have not chosen this ministry. It has been given to us by a higher source. Had we our way, we would have opened a lucrative chiropractic office. Instead, we are treading the straight and narrow path of sacrificial service. Please fill out the enclosed card before the ground freezes over, and make your check payable to Linda Emery Ministries.

Unabashedly,

Linda Emery

Linda Emery,
President

By Linda S. Emery

From Issue #58/December, 1980–January, 1981

Linda Emery Ministries
P.O. Box 3867
Eugene, Oregon 94702
Phone (please): (561) 555-8126

RIGHT: From Issue #54/April–May, 1980; BELOW: From Issue #46/December, 1978–January, 1979

Mongolians rarely become bald. The same is true of American Indians.

More than 90 percent of flowers have either an unpleasant odor or none at all.

It's against the law to make a pastry reproduction of the White House.

There are more psychiatrists per person in Washington, D.C. than anywhere else.

You burn up 3 and a half calories every time you laugh.

7

The Body Part That Helps You Keep Your Balance When You Lean too Far Back in Your Chair and Almost Tip Over

Cults, Splits, and Factions

A lot of falling goes on in the Bible. Adam and Eve were the first to fall when they ate the forbidden fruit in the Garden of Eden. As a result, men were cursed with difficult work and women got stuck with dominating husbands, painful childbirth, and long lines at public rest rooms.

In the New Testament, there is continued emphasis on falling. Paul says we must be sensitive to the beliefs of young Christians so they don't stumble and fall. Even if a certain behavior is not inherently wrong, he says we should avoid it if it might cause our "weaker brother" to stumble. My neighbor Clarence says we should also avoid behavior that causes a "stronger brother" to skip in public or a "clumsy brother" to lean too far back in his chair, feel a moment of panic, and almost tip over.

Although it is usually a good idea to ignore Clarence, he has a point when he talks about the need for balance, so that's what this chapter is about.

Our physical sense of balance is maintained by a bunch of bony loops in the inner ear; when these get out of kilter, the world seems to spin and we lose our stability. When that happens, falling becomes routine.

The Door has had a knack for identifying some of the reasons that our spiritual lives get out of kilter, causing us to tumble into sin. In particular, it has focused on why some people stumble and fall into cults. *The Door* was the first periodical to expose the shallowness of that classic New Age book *I'm a god, So Shut Up!* In it, Dr. Tex Majanda says we are all gods, which looks great on a resume but doesn't impress God all that much.

Cults are certainly not the only trap waiting for out-of-balance enthusiasts to fall into. *The Door* has also examined some of the ways that people within the church fall victim to divisions, in-fighting, and concessions to culture. Therefore, this chapter will also take us into the realm of splits, factions, and other out-of-balance off-shoots of the church.

Trying to keep our spiritual balance is anything but boring. As G. K. Chesterton wrote, "It is always simple to fall; there are an infinity of angles at which one falls, only one at which one stands. To have fallen into any one of the fads from Gnosticism to Christian Science would indeed have been obvious and tame. But to have avoided them all has been one whirling adventure; and in my vision the heavenly chariot flies thundering through the ages, the dull heresies sprawling and prostrate, the wild truth reeling but erect."

HARE KRISHNA TO YOU,
HARE KRISHNA TO YOU,
HARE KRISHNA, DEAR HOWARD,
HARE KRISHNA TO YOU!

From Issue #59/February–March, 1981

OUT
IN *LiMBO*

By J. Yutaka Amano

From Double Issue #98–99/August–September–October–November, 1987

Actress, singer, and dancer, Shirley MacLaine, in 1983, revealed her alleged reincarnation experiences in her best- seller, Out on a Limb. *These explorations were taken to a deeper level in another best-seller,* Dancing in the Light *(1985). In early 1987, ABC aired a mini-series based on these Eastern excursions. But the interpretation of any tale lies in the eyes of its teller.*

*S*tepping into one of the famous Andes mineral baths sparked a cold, tingling sensation inside of me. After all, this was where humanity and divinity intertwine. Where souls escape the bondage of bodily baggage and become one with the Universal Soul.

Out in the middle of the pool hovered a mystic candle. Rings of light emanated from it, with swirls of smoke forming a spiral staircase to the heavens. My eyes were irresistibly drawn towards the flame. Its flickering light fingered its way through the midnight air and bathed me in its warmth. Soon I was transfixed by its brilliant display of colors. The light seemed to glow all about me. I was achieving union. In one orgasmic flash, I had become one with the candle flame.

The next day, I awoke in a primitive Peruvian hospital—being treated for third-degree burns. It seems my union with the flame was more literal than I had expected.

Dauntless, I soon resumed my incessant quest for spiritual enlightenment. Climbing atop one of the highest points in Peru on a beautiful starlit night, I meditated in one of the primary centers for UFO activity.

Extraterrestrials are far more advanced than we are, spiritually as well as intellectually. Further along in the evolutionary process, ETs are much more in tune with cosmic realities. That's why I've always been eager to search the celestial heavens for that one divine glimpse—to reach out and touch some alien force which could speed up my journey toward spiritual perfection.

That night my prayers were answered. As I gazed into the heavens, I felt an unearthly presence. I knew intuitively, without the slightest hint of visual contact, that an ET was standing behind me. Unafraid, I slowly turned to face my spiritual leader.

"Lady, you wanna buy some baskets?" asked the ET.

ETs are known for changing their forms at will. This particular creature from outer space obviously felt that the form of a Mayan Indian woman would be the least offensive to me. I wanted to assure her that we were on the same wavelength.

"It's all right," I said. "You can be straight with me. Show me your true form."

"Well, I got both thick and thin weave baskets. I make myself. Good stuff, eh? You have two dolla?"

ETs are so esoteric. You have to get behind the literal, obvious meaning of the words in order to understand the deeper, spiritual truths they intend to convey. With every fiber of my aerobicized being, I knew that the baskets represented our bodies—bodies of all sizes and shapes.

"Look, if you no like your basket and change your mind, I'll give you another one," she said.

I couldn't believe my ears. Here I was, half a world away from home, and I had just witnessed confirmation from an advanced being of the doctrine of reincarnation. Each basket—that is, each body—is only used when suitable for our potential. Then we change bodies. That is, reincarnation occurs to further our development. Never had I heard such wisdom, such insight, with such clarity.

"Hey, maybe you tell your friends about me and I give them some baskets too. You nice, pretty lady. Tell friends now, okee-dokee?"

As she turned to leave, I realized the great yet wonderful responsibility laid on my shoulders. This advanced being had chosen me to be the prophet of the New Age. I was to herald the doctrine of reincarnation to the Western world.

Realizing my awesome task, it occurred to me that I needed more train-ing about this ancient doctrine. Within a few days, I arrived in northern India seeking out a guru who would give me insight into the wonders of Eastern recycling. In India, there are millions of people and hundreds of gurus. How does one go about finding her spiritual teacher? Through great care, prayer, and devotion; through meditation, preparation, and the constellations. Why, through the Yellow pages, of course!

My search led me to one Guru Levi-Gene. "Hello enlightened master," I said. "May I seek your spiritual consultation?"

"Oh definitely. That'll be five bucks."

"Uh, pardon me, but you don't sound like a guru."

"I'm a Ph.D. in physics, a scientific investigator of hallucinogens, and a guide to urbanite mysticism. Whaddya wanna know?"

Contrary to my thoughts at the time, I had to trust my spiritual intuition. "Well, I need to know why the world needs to embrace the doctrine of reincarnation."

"Wow, that's a heavy one, but easy enough to answer," he said. "Reincarnation is necessary for us to understand the workings of cosmic justice."

"Cosmic justice?"

"Yeah, cosmic justice. Why does an innocent kid die of starvation? Why are babies born deformed? Why do good people suffer and bad people prosper? Why will the IRS haul my carcass into the slammer if I show my face in the States?"

"OK, what you're saying is that reincarnation involves the notion of 'karma'—which is simply the law of cause and effect. Karma says that the deeds you perform in one life will determine your life in another reincarnation. So, do you mean reincarnation solves the problem of earthly suffering by explaining the universal fact that we must all one day pay our dues, whether in this life or another?"

"Gee, I hope not. I'm not planning on going back to the U.S."

"Then there are loopholes in the reincarnation system?"

"Loopholes!? That's how I got in trouble with the IRS in the first place!"

I could see that I needed to focus my spiritual energies with a little more discernment. This was no guru.

After several days of wandering around, I found an authentic guru. Anyone could see that his dark skin, long, matted hair, and charisma with the village flies certified him as a bona fide guru. His long hours of meditation were evidenced by the rhythmic, nasally rumble emanating from the center of his being. Less enlightened westerners might confuse this mystical sight for snoring.

"Spiritual master," I cried out, "tell me how reincarnation can save our world."

"Ah, my child. If reincarnation is true, then we are all one. Each of us has been the other in some life long past. All males have been, at one time or another, females; Jews have been Gentiles; whites, black; Christians, Buddhist . . . "

"Hindus, Muslim?"

"No! Never in a thousand moons! Blacken the day when—"

"OK, OK, I'm sorry already."

"Humph. As I was saying, reincarnation demonstrates that we are all one. Therefore, there is no need for fighting and intolerance—"

"What you're saying is—"

"Silence! Interrupt me not!" Clearing his throat, he proceeded. "As I was saying, rather than extending the

hand in violence, one will extend the warmth of universal love."

"I see. Oh my, who's that lying beside you? He looks half-dead."

"He probably is. He's been like that for weeks."

"Why don't you call a doctor?"

"My child, the reason for his suffering is his misdeeds in a former life. Who am I to interfere with karmic justice?"

"But what you said about universal love . . . "

"Look, white eyes, if I help him, then I would only be tampering with the unbreakable law of karma, which would not only make him suffer all the more in a future life, but screw up my destiny as well!"

"Then how can we extend the concept of universal love if it'll only disrupt universal justice?"

"Life is a paradox, is it not? In spiritual reality, contradictions abound, free of rational restraints. The finite is infinite; the temporal, eternal; the right, wrong. Free your mind of questions. Unchain yourself from the shackles of reason. Become one with all things. Attain unity at all costs."

Funny. I was reminded of the candle flame.

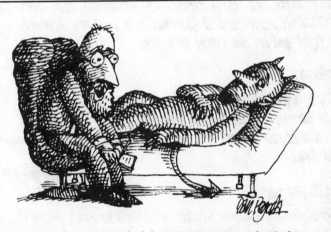

"Whether I or anyone else believes in you anymore is beside the point. The important thing is that you believe in yourself."

TOP: From Issue #59/February–March, 1981; CENTER: From Issue #74/August–September, 1983 RIGHT: From Issue #74/August–September, 1983;

The Devil Takes Cuts in Line at the Movies

GET BEHIND ME, SATAN

JIM McBEAVER'S TRIBULATION SURVIVAL DIARY

JUNE 3RD 1987

Morning news said Russian Bear finally moving on Israel. We quickly fled to Colorado mountains. This is THE BIG SHOW!

JUNE 4TH 1987

Supplies are untouched: seven years of food, Bible video games, old PTL tapes, low altitude radar, biological warfare antidotes, radiation suits, 12 M-16 rifles, 23 Sidewinder heat-seeking anti-personnel missles and 8 bazookas with rockets. Now we can sit tight and let the storm blow over.

JUNE 5 1987

Much discussion about outsiders. Disgruntled pre-tribbers would be harmful. It was agreed that those who think exactly as we do could become hewers and drawers of water. Also agreed that I should lead.

JULY 4TH 1987

Some foolishly question whether we should be here, calling it monasticism. I won the argument because I know I am right.

JULY 15, 1987

Stranger sighted. Looked like the type who would stamp a number on you. I got him in my sights and wasted him.

JULY 17TH 1987

Small herd of non-elect wandering nearby. Three bucks and two does. We readied for battle but they wandered off. Later that day, we adopted 'No pearls before swine' as our motto.

AUGUST 3RD 1987

We found a seven year old girl wandering alone, starving and terrified. After lengthy consultations, prayer and a close vote, we decided to take hen in. She'll be my wife's maid servant.

AUGUST 26th 1987

Big trouble. Marauding band of secular humanists, pantheists and hedonists. Missiles were readied, but they didn't find us. One of them had a Swiss army knife. I could've used. Handy little things in the bush.

SEPTEMBER 8th 1987   While foraging by a river, I found a dead pack of theological liberals. Fools! They had my books! Slim pickings here: small radio, volume of Barth and some Foster Grants that I now wear all the time.

SEPTEMBER 19th 1987
                                    outside   strong
Desires to investigate the world are, among us. I quash them.

❀ OCTOBER 2nd 1987

Two of us left this morning. They have no chance. Oh well, more food for the rest of us. Less than 7 years to go now. We can hold on if we trust only in God and not in our own strength.

NOVEMBER 1st 1987   Sighted singer John Denver. Scared him off with a burst. "Hey," he said, "Don't you know who I am?!" I answered "Yeah, you Oriental mystic, go find some Hare Krishnas!" Then he screamed out. "WHAT DID I DO WRONG?" That was easy, "I don't like your music!" I said. That country boy can sure run!

NOVEMBER 14th 1987   Cold setting in. Radio blasts out lies all day. I am not fooled. We are ready to die here if necessary.

DECEMBER 12th 1987

Typhoid outbreak. Several dead. Outlook bleak. Medicine gone. I thought we had everything.

DECEMBER 20th 1987 I'm the last one left and slipping fast. LORD HELP ME. HANG on until you come !! Make sure the radar and missiles work if I am attacked.

DECEMBER 25th 1987

Snowy Christmas morning. Inter-Church World Rescue Team found me. They confirmed that the new Mid-East treaty has been signed and hostilities have ceased. They asked me some tough questions about backpackers in the area. So I was wrong. We all make mistakes.

By Lloyd Billingsley

From Issue #63/October–November 1981

» **Video psychiatry.** In *Talk to Me* (Concord Video, $9.95, 30 minutes, due in fall), a therapist asks, "How do you feel?" and "Would you like to expand on that?," pausing for replies.

» **New Age help.** *Shirley Mac-Laine: Healing Within* (Vestron, $29.98, 60 minutes, February) takes an existential tour of the body. Says MacLaine: "Aligning your body is as important as working out."

ABOVE: From Issue #104/March–April, 1989;
RIGHT: From Issue #104/March–April, 1989;
BELOW: From Issue #56/August–September, 1980

August 25, 1980

Church fight erupts; police cancel service

MOUNT CLEMENS (AP) — Police canceled a Sunday worship service after fighting broke out in the congregation over who should be pastor at the Greater Morning Star Baptist Church.

Five Mount Clemens police officers and Macomb County sheriff's deputies were called to break up the disturbance.

During the service, two rival ministers — the Rev. Nathaniel Calhoun and the Rev. Clarenton Bullock — stood in the pulpit using separate microphones.

While Calhoun led his group of church members in the reading of Psalm 122, Bullock and his followers tried to outshout them with a reading of Psalm 92.

UNDER AN AGREEMENT negotiated between the factions, each group's minister was supposed to preach on alternate Sundays.

It was Bullock's turn on Sunday, but Calhoun told the congregation he was claiming the pulpit "because I was elected your pastor and I'm supposed to preach."

Alexander Miner Jr., 21,

of Mount Clemens, told police that Rose Nelson walked up to his pew and grabbed his face with her hand before the service began. Miner said he tried to free himself from her grasp, but Erskine Nelson, the woman's son, hit him on the head. Miner said he supports Calhoun. Mrs. Nelson declined to comment. Shouts and threats interrupted the service until Sgt. B.A. Campau of the Mount Clemens police department walked up the aisle and told the congregation to go home.

Preacher says he'll barbecue Good News Bible

DENVER (UPI) — The Rev. Maurice Gordon will use his barbecue grill to burn a copy of the Good News Bible next week because he believes it misinterprets Scripture and is "more insulting than pornography."

The minister, pastor of the Lovingway Church, describes himself as a "primitive Christian." He planned to give away copies of the traditional King James Bible to any of his 100 to 200 parishioners attending the Dec. 19 burning.

The minister said he will use a barbecue grill to burn the Bible because the city prohibited open burning.

"I blame it on Satan who wants to sidetrack people by changing what they read," said the Rev. Mr. Gordon. He said young persons reading new translations were "being led subtly astray like the Pied Piper of Hamlin."

Looking for a church - Ind., Fund., Premill., Pretrib., Disp., nondenominational, nonsectarian, noncharismatic, evangelistic, missionary with biblical separation, non-legalistic, calvinistic but not hyper, emphasizing The Church (all believers) and the local church. Pastor's job church govern., ordinances, not extra biblical. Leave name and phone number at 327-0606.   HP24P

Correction

Joint worship does not include all Lutherans

A story in the Saturday Missoulian reported that the Lutheran and Roman Catholic parishes of Missoula will participate in a joint worship celebrating Reformation Sunday, on Sunday at St. Paul's Lutheran Church.

The joint worship will include Missoula parishes of the American Lutheran Church and the Lutheran Church in America, but not parishes of the Missouri and Wisconsin synods.

ABOVE: From Issue #71/February–March, 1983; ABOVE RIGHT: From Issue #65/February–March, 1982; RIGHT: From Issue #68/August–September, 1982

Interesting
NEW
CHURCHES

By Chuck Westerman

From Issue #88/December, 1985–
January, 1986

**The Mortin R. Meldrim
Congregational Church**

Whitefield held services in a field, and people scoffed. Finney preached in tents and was mocked. Schuller opened a drive-in church and everyone said, "Hey, a drive-in church. What a nut."

But the skeptics were proven wrong. Whitefield thrived. Finney reached thousands. And Schuller's church is still the only one that teenagers have ever tried to sneak into by locking themselves into the trunk of a '74 Skylark.

New forms of religious expression will continue to emerge. Here are a few appearing on the horizon.

First Church of Christ Teleconference

Every Sunday morning at 11 a.m., Eastern Standard Time, over 600 members and regular attenders dial a toll-free 800 number, push the # button on their Touch-Tones, and are thus connected to the only church service in America conducted by phone.

Bulletins mailed out the previous week allow worshippers to follow the liturgy without ever getting out of their beds. Visa and MasterCard numbers are used to collect the offering, and Prayer and Share circles are organized according to area code. A "Call Waiting" feature allows worshippers who are gifted with prophecy to deliver a direct Word of God in the middle of the sermon.

Currently, the Justice Department is trying to break up the Church into a number of competing fellowships, and to force the F.C.C.T. to divest itself of its youth ministries. It is unclear at this time whether Constitutional religious safeguards or federal antitrust statutes take precedence.

The Mobile Baptist Church

Mobile as in "auto-" rather than "Alabama." The church is housed entirely in a tractor-trailer-sized recreational vehicle that makes a regular circuit of Indiana and Ohio. Worshippers board for the 9 o'clock service in Evansville, and for the eleven o'clock service just north of Peducah, Kentucky. Midweek prayer meetings are scheduled as road construction patterns permit.

Youth Sunday School classes run concurrently with adult worship and are held in a fleet of Ford mini-vans that keep pace with the Mother Church. Rest stops generally fall between the Reading of the Lesson and the Offertory Solo.

Members are, at this time, looking for a trailer park into which they can settle—partly because gas mileage isn't what it used to be and partly because they're tired of answering the question, "Where is your church?" with "I just saw it roll by an hour ago; it's probably twenty-five miles on down I-65 by now."

Rambo Revisionist Temple

The result of an "unreached people group" mission strategy, this congregation is made up entirely of M.I.A.'s who were rescued from Vietnam in the movies *Uncommon Valor*, *Missing in Action I and II*, *Rambo*, etc.

Services are held on a Hollywood back lot and feature creative liturgies:

Leader: God be wit' you.
Troops: An' wit' you.
Leader: We coulda won the war . . .
Troops: . . . If those lousy politicians hadda let us.

Sermons are based on a Bible that has been reduced to battle passages from the Pentateuch and a smattering of imprecatory verses from the Psalms.

During special fellowship hours, attenders relive cinematic revenge fantasies against demonic Orientals who can't stand up to the bravery of American special forces armed with helicopters, flamethrowers, movie bullets, and a feeble historical memory.

Spin-off temples will work with other "unreached people groups" like all the American freedom fighters killed in *Red Dawn* and *Invasion U.S.A.*, and all the blacks who wished they could have stayed slaves in *Gone With the Wind* and *Birth of a Nation*.

The Agape Boat

Less a church than a combined evangelistic mission and floating counseling center, the Agape Boat ministers to fading character actors, game show celebrities who have been unemployed since *Hollywood Squares* went off the air, and Charo.

Church membership is easily obtained but expires at the end of the week. Services are held on Saturday nights at 10 o'clock (9 o'clock Central and Pacific time).

Observers of the Agape Boat's ministry report remarkable accomplishments. Records show a 100-percent success rate in solving even the most intractable of religious crises over the course of a five-day cruise. The pastoral style of the ship's staff (characterized in ministerial manuals as "wacky but lovable") appears to foster in passengers the development of increased life-meaning, spiritual maturity, and improved skin tone.

The Mortin R. Meldrim Congregational Church

Vowing that "Nobody's going to tell *me* what to believe or how to live my life," Mort Meldrim broke away from the Church of Christ-Meldrim Family in 1982 to form his own church and denomination, of which he is the sole member.

While little is known about the M.R.M.C.C.'s operation or doctrine, rumors have surfaced that factions forming within the church may lead to another split in the near future. This would be unusual, but is not unprecedented. In 1965, an Arizona man who had formed a single-member church was diagnosed with a multiple-identity disorder. Within two years, each of his other six personalities had started its own sect, and two had made down-payments on satellite dishes.

The Irony of Fundamentalism

By Ben Patterson

From Issue #70/December, 1982–January, 1983

A church split a few years ago over a doctrinal issue I have long since forgotten. They had managed to hold together until an itinerant evangelist came to conduct a revival. When told of their difficulties, he decided to preach a sermon on Paul's split with Barnabas. You will recall, the two men parted company because they could not agree on Mark's suitability to travel with them on a missionary journey. The preacher took that to mean that God felt it was okay for churches to split. Instead of an altar call that night, they had a business meeting to formally divide the church.

The history of the fundamentalist movement is shot through with ironies, of which that event is a paradigm. In its efforts to preserve the integrity of the one Church under one Lord and proclaiming one Gospel, it has accomplished nearly the opposite, time and time again. It appears that wherever fundamentalism raises its banner, there will be a plethora of churches instead of one church, all claiming to be the one true church, or at the very least, the truest of the lot. Fundamentalism's zeal for the truth of the Bible has more often than not splintered and divided the Church of the Bible.

The movement has always been centrifugal. A pastor, a seminary, a professor, a church, or a denomination will not adhere to the fundamentals of the faith as defined by the fundamentalist, or in the way the fundamentalist feels they should be adhered to. One by one, they go flying off helter-skelter in every direction, amid accusations and allegations and recriminations. The things that should unite Christians—the Gospel, the sacraments, and the Bible—become occasions for what divide Christians.

The fundamentalist is forever squinting his eyes and looking you over to find something wrong with the way you live or think. He wants to know not, do you believe the Bible, but do you *really* believe the Bible? His concern is not, are you a Christian, but are you a *born-again* Christian? That attitude spells death for the Christian fellowship. There simply cannot be meaningful fellowship when everyone is being gone over with theological white gloves. Thus, fundamentalism breaks up the holy catholic Church and the communion of saints it seeks to hold intact.

There is another irony in the fundamentalist movement. It is so preoccupied with teaching its adherents what to think, that it forgets to teach them how to think. The result is that they often lose their ability to know what to think as well. Case in point: John Feinberg, the chairman of the Department of Theological Studies at Liberty Baptist Seminary, wrote an article for *The Fundamentalist Journal* about the dilemmas posed by conflicting demands for authority in the Christian's life. He opened with what he claimed was the true story of a Christian woman, a born-again Christian woman, a fundamentalist Christian woman. Being all of the above, she sought conscientiously to be obedient and submissive to her husband. Unfortunately, her husband was not a believer. Not only that, but he was a particularly unscrupulous pagan who insisted that his wife give sexual favors to potential business clients. What was the poor woman to do? Was she to obey God and be submissive to her husband, and at the same time disobey God and commit adultery?

Mr. Feinberg wrote with great vigor and compassion as he sought to show that she should, in this case, disobey her husband in order to obey God. Of course! What left me befuddled was the fact that the dilemma should have arisen in the first place. In other words, it is sad to be married to such a jerk, but it is also sad to be taught by your pastors and theologians to think so rigidly. When life is conceived in such wooden, black and white terms, it gives birth to all kinds of false dilemmas. It struck me, as I read theologian Feinberg's response, that what he really needed to do was to teach wives and other fundamentalists not only what to think about the faith, but also *how* to think about the faith.

Whenever I think of fundamentalism, I think of charts and lists and systems, and equations. I think of Jerry Falwell chanting, "If it is old, it is true; if it is new, it is not true." I also think of the fact that I grew up in a fundamentalist church, and that I am very grateful for what I received there. I learned my Bible. (Did I ever learn my Bible! I could have passed my seminary comprehensives in Old and New Testament content my first year of college, because of what my fundamentalist Sunday School did for me.) I learned the importance of discipline in the Church. I learned that Christians needed to see themselves as separate from the world. I learned the fundamentals! I still believe the fundamentals. Indeed, I would be a poorer man today if I had not grown up in a church that was a member of the Independent Fundamental Churches of America, which advertised on its billboard: "We Preach the Book, the Blood, and the Blessed Hope."

Then why am I no longer in one of those churches? Mainly because somewhere along the line I learned from the same Bible that Christ also loved the Church and "gave Himself for her, that He might present her spotless." I learned that Christ loved the Church not because she was spotless, but that He might make her that way. He loved her in hope, and so should I. It is important for me to be in a church like the United Presbyterian Church, mainline denomination, member of the infamous World Council of Churches, and ridiculously pluralistic. I am forced almost daily to make a decision to love people who espouse positions I do not agree with, and at times find abhorrent. It is important for me to do that because I believe that is what Jesus Himself is doing . . . for all of us, including the fundamentalists.

If I could mandate anything for the fundamentalist movement, I would mandate that outlook. It is certainly my prayer for it: that it would love the Church of the Bible as much as it loves the Bible, and be willing to enter into serious dialogue and cooperation with other Christians who do not dot all of their "i's" and cross all of their "t's" as it

does. It would thaw a lot of frozen minds to do so. Ed Dobson and Ed Hindson, co-authors of the book, *The Fundamentalist Phenomenon*, acknowledge as a weakness the movement's small capacity for self-criticism. But will they acknowledge as weakness also, the movement's total refusal to be criticized by those outside of it—by liberals and Roman Catholics and by evangelicals?

Both fundamentalists and the rest of us are likely to be filled with surprises when we see God's final assessment of what we championed here on earth. In fact, we'd better get used to the fact that we will be spending eternity together, so we should probably learn to get along with each other before that time comes. Otherwise, heaven may turn out to not be so heavenly after all.

From Issue #73/June–July, 1983

By Christopher Carlisle

From Issue #89/February–March, 1986

church of the young urban professional

Ministers of the Church have long been plagued with the problem of making the institution relevant and palatable to the contemporary scene. Responsible ones have been known to give up their precious vacation Sunday mornings for a rare chance to sample other houses of worship which might reveal secrets to this end.

It was up on the West Side—Columbus Avenue, I think . . .

Between two commercial establishments (The Great Expectations Health Club and the little eatery, The Grey Poupon Sushi Bar) stood a lovely renovated brownstone which bore a sign out front:

> **Church of the Young Urban**
> **Professional**
> *Sunday Conferencing*
> *8:00 and 10:00 A.M.*
> *Holy Communion*

Taking a seat in the back, I was immediately struck with the Church's first concession to the times. There were no wooden pews here. Rather, carefully arranged clusters of sectional sofas gave the room a quiet reminiscence of the furniture floor at Bloomingdale's. I picked up the Sunday Bulletin on the end table next to me and, beneath the soft glow of the track lighting, I began to survey the order of worship.

Several items at the bottom of the bulletin caught my attention:

1. The hanging plants are given in loving memory of Spencer Grayson, recently departed for a promotion in Chicago.
2. This morning's communion wine is a Cabernet Sauvignon, 1976.
3. The Dow Jones closed on the Feast of St. Francis at 1278, up six and one-half points.

Aside from my not being clad in a jogging suit, I felt quite at home. The Rector was one of those handsome, faintly familiar fellows who smiled a great deal, spoke most often "on the other hand," and winked every time he mentioned "corporate worship." At the communion rail, I noticed he was wearing a button-down clerical collar with his initials monogrammed around the bend.

Indeed, the entire service was given to just two uncomfortable moments. For those raised on American currency pledging, the credit card machine screwed into the offering plate was a surprise. And, at the end of the sermon, the congregation assumed the unanticipated format of breaking into small groups to exchange business cards, job openings, and several rounds of Trivial Pursuit. As I glanced again at the Sunday bulletin, I noted that the word "sermon" had been replaced by the term "networking."

At the close of the service, the Rector extended a cordial invitation to "brunch downstairs in the Sunday School room." As no one in the congregation appeared to be the sort to have children, I was not surprised to find the room's name to be a leftover description for what was now a small art gallery exhibiting twentieth-century French lithographs for under five hundred dollars. The buffet—an impressive array of duck-liver pate, escargots, stuffed mushroom caps, kiwi fruit, croissants, and chocolate cheesecake—

was a further opportunity to talk about Spencer Grayson and his new life in Chicago.

The Rector stood at the front door, greeting people (as only rectors can) and promoting the church's one-day pilgrimage to the Holy Land with week-long stopovers in Paris and London. It was then that his identity came back to me. He was the priest who had gained wide notoriety in the country-club heyday of the 1950s when he instituted his novel liturgical rite: "The Blessing of the Golf Carts."

From Issue #102/April–May, 1988

COMPUFEL

Revolutionary High-Tech Fellowship *An interview with Dr. M. Chip Newbyte*

By Daniel Kain

From Issue #79/June–July, 1984

DOOR: Dr. Newbyte, what got you started on high-tech fellowship?

NEWBYTE: I would have to identify three main elements here. First, divine guidance. I always operate under the direction of God. Second, a computer salesman. We were talking one day and, in the most casual manner (not knowing he was a Balaam's ass), the man said, "Gee, it's a shame to see the Church fall so far behind modern technology."

DOOR: And you think he spoke from God?

NEWBYTE: I pondered it long and hard, indeed. Businesses use computers. Homes and schools use computers. Even the government uses computers. The Church should be the engineer, not sitting in the caboose.

DOOR: You said there were three things.

NEWBYTE: Yes.

DOOR: Well?

NEWBYTE: So we developed a computer organization for our small group meetings.

DOOR: And how was that arranged?

NEWBYTE: Originally, we purchased just one computer using group donations. I offered to keep it at my home, and then the brothers and sisters could come over to run their programs.

DOOR: What sort of things were you running?

NEWBYTE: Oh, attendance statistics, tax shelters, missionary allotments, hymnal wear and tear—the usual sort of church business. But we found that one computer wasn't enough.

DOOR: Yes. And it must have been a hardship having all those people in your home. Is the fellowship large?

NEWBYTE: Yes. Four families. Three now, actually.

DOOR: And what changes resulted from your purchasing the additional computers?

NEWBYTE: Innumerable ones. First, I didn't have to hide the game cartridges anymore. Second, our worship improved.

DOOR: Really? Why was that?

NEWBYTE: Synthesized hymns. I developed the program for it myself. No more flat voices, no more rushed choruses. The computer does it all for us.

DOOR: That would be more exact.

NEWBYTE: Certainly. The monks should have had synthesizers for their Gregorian chants—that might have forestalled rock music altogether. Then there was the guidance program.

DOOR: What was that?

NEWBYTE: Oh, just a little aid we

whipped up. Did you know that a computer can consider every option available to a single human being in about one forty-thousandth of a second?

DOOR: That's fast!

NEWBYTE: I'll bet you can't get that fast an answer by praying. And that reminds me of something else. We process all prayers on a program we call LORD—Lots of Oral Requests to Deity.

DOOR: And how does that work?

NEWBYTE: Really well.

DOOR: We were asking if you could explain the process.

NEWBYTE: Sure. Actually, there are three key aspects to our reasoning here. First, you know how often you end up repeating a prayer? Our LORD files have over 78,000 prayers on memory right now. We can just download the appropriate prayer and flash it on the display screen for God to see. Say you need a noon blessing for a vegetarian lunch during that hectic week before Halloween. Just punch in the data, turn the display heavenward, and dig in. Second, we're working on a system that will match prayers with answers from our LORD data-base. We hope to see the day when prayers are fulfilled on the video display screen before they materialize elsewhere.

DOOR: A sort of electronic prophet?

NEWBYTE: No, we don't want to make any money on this. It's the Lord's work.

DOOR: Has your move to high-tech affected the group relationships?

NEWBYTE: Certainly. We are able to share more easily than ever.

DOOR: Why is that?

NEWBYTE: Telephone terminals. Let's say I'm not feeling well. I type the specifics into my computer. Anyone else in the fellowship can call up the file on me and see that I have a need. They then run the LORD program, which locates a suitable prayer, and they can be popping corn while the intercession rises to heaven. And we don't even have to talk.

DOOR: Your system could save words, theoretically—

NEWBYTE: Oh, more than that. COMPUFEL—Computer Fellowship—saves far more than words. I have the best fellowship that I've ever had, and I don't need to use gas, money, time, coffee, or cookies.

DOOR: That's amazing! How?

NEWBYTE: Why, I haven't seen a member of my group in over eight months. We log on, download, interface, and synthesize. We don't have to get together. We don't ever see each other.

DOOR: Isn't that a little—

NEWBYTE: Of course. A little miracle. A little end to all conflict. We never dispute or haggle over endless genealogies, as the Scripture says. We don't rub each other wrong. We have the most sanitary sanctification imaginable.

DOOR: You never disagree?

NEWBYTE: Never. Our theological differences are run through the THEO program: Theological disHarmony Extractions Operative. There are no struggles over meat offered to idols. THEO tells us what to do.

DOOR: And THEO can handle even the really big questions—like predestination?

NEWBYTE: What will be, will be. We don't have to think about it.

DOOR: Do you see any implications for the Church at large?

NEWBYTE: Naturally. There will come a time when computers will replace all the less efficient elements of church. For instance, the pastor will be one of the first things to go—right after the organist. Then there's the monthly business meeting. Oh, and missionary drives.

DOOR: How will we finance missionaries?

NEWBYTE: We won't. We won't need them. All we'll need is one terminal with a large video display screen in every village. There'll be no more wasteful trips. We're calling the system the "Apostle POL"—People On Line.

DOOR: And you don't think the missing "human" factor is important?

NEWBYTE: People make mistakes. Computers are inerrant. Besides, did you ever drink the water in those places?

DOOR: Well—uh—

NEWBYTE: Computers are the coming thing. You mark my word. I've already got a franchise for a chain of Christian computer stores.

DOOR: And you'll sell—

NEWBYTE: Everything. Hardware. Software, which we'll be calling "soulware."

DOOR: What's your chain called?

NEWBYTE: Floppy Disks for Jesus.

DOOR: Interesting. But is all this Scriptural?

NEWBYTE: You bet. We have many Scriptures to support us. The most important is Luke 17:24. Remember it?

DOOR: Uh—

NEWBYTE: It's about the Second Coming. "For just as the lightning, when it flashes out of one part of the sky, shines to the other part of the sky, so will the Son of Man be in His day." Only one way to do that: computer graphics.

DOOR: So there's no stopping a computerized Church?

NEWBYTE: Absolutely not. It's been coming since the opening pages of Genesis. Eve just bit into the wrong kind of Apple. 🔑

8

The Wrinkly Skin on the Elbow

A Hodgepodge

For years I have wondered what function is served by the wrinkly skin on our elbows. In college, one of my wife's girlfriends used to kiss my elbows (this is true), so I often wondered whether the wrinkly skin was there to attract members of the opposite sex, like the feathers displayed by a peacock. (The main difference is that more tourists run for their cameras when a peacock shows its feathers than when I display my elbows.)

As I thought more and more about my elbows, I came to realize that the wrinkly skin symbolizes life itself. Think about it. Just as I have often wondered what purpose is served by the wrinkly skin, humans have often asked themselves, "What are we doing on Planet Earth? Why are we here? What is our ultimate purpose (besides the fact that somebody has to clean out the kitty litter boxes or the planet would soon be uninhabitable)?"

Believe it or not, even *The Door* has asked itself these ultimate questions. Back in 1987 a reader wrote, "*The Door* is history. It is time to cease publication. . . . One form of institutionalism is the carrying on of a program which has outlived its purpose. To continue to publish *The Door* would be to prostitute yourselves."

This letter sent many on *The Door* staff into a mid-life crisis. To give you an idea of how serious that letter was taken, here is how the Doorkeepers sized up the situation in Issue #87:

"This particular letter was the one that caused us to go over the edge into a full-blown, mid-life crisis. We found ourselves coming to work listless and unable to concentrate. We began second-guessing everything we were doing. Maybe *The Door* does need to cease publishing forever—or at least for a few months—but if we do that, who will notice? Maybe we need to change our image. Maybe we need to become more angry, or more spiritual, or more liberal, or more . . . uh . . . more professional.

"In desperation, we decided to spend a few days at a retreat for burned-out magazines. It was a magazine-changing experience. There, in the solitude of the giant printing presses, everything came back in focus. We realized that we could never be another *Moody Monthly* (no, one *Moody Monthly* is enough). Neither could we become a Christian punk magazine—none of us have any hair. We realized we couldn't become liberals either. (Yes, we have the pipes and beards, but we just can't stomach the Father-Mother God stuff.)

"It took us awhile but, after hours of deep introspection and soul-searching, we came upon a great truth: *The Door* must go on. It has to go on for one simple, but profound reason—we need the work. Yes, it was as though a voice spoke to us out of the darkness and said, 'If you jerks worked for anyone else, you would be fired.' We knew then that *The Door* had to keep going."

This book has to keep going as well. So let's move to the final chapter—a variety of pieces that didn't quite fit any of the other chapters. You might say that these articles went through a similar identity crisis, wondering if they really fit in this book, wondering if they are as useless as the wrinkly skin on our elbows.

But just as all of us serve a purpose on earth, I think these pieces serve a purpose too. I'm not sure what that purpose is, but if you leave your phone number, I'll call you as soon as I discover it.

In the meantime, *The Door* continues publishing. It has to. For as one reader expressed it, "A day without *The Door* is like a day without an ulcer."

Uh . . . thanks.

The Tear

By Dan Pegoda

From Issue #50/
August–September, 1979

"How are things going, Al?" Al played second base.

"Oh, not bad, considering my wife just filed for a divorce. You're batting ninth in the lineup tonight, Wayne."

"You're JOKING . . . about the divorce, that is."

He wasn't joking. I was shocked. I had known Albert and Donna for almost six years and I never even had a clue anything was wrong. I needed more information, so during the bottom of the third inning, I sat down on the bench next to Al. He was pretty open about it.

"Everything was just fine—at least I thought it was—until about three years ago," he said. "It was at that couples retreat in Palm Springs that we had our first real fight. Charlie Shedd was the speaker, and he said that a happy marriage is a marriage where people really talk a lot. Well, Donna started complaining that I don't talk enough. You know what I mean?"

"I think so."

"A few months later, the men's group at the church did a study using Larry Christianson's book, *The Christian Family*. One of the things we learned from that study is that wives are supposed to submit to their husbands. So, I told Donna that God wanted her to start submitting a little more."

"She didn't go for that, huh?"

"No way. But I was only suggesting it as a way to improve our marriage. The book almost guaranteed that it would. But then, I doubt that Christianson had ever met anyone like Donna."

"Probably not."

"I guess the next real crisis was when Donna ordered some tapes by a guy named Barley or Wheat or something, on sexual fulfillment in marriage. You know Donna—she's always had a lusty side to her. Anyway, after getting all turned on by those tapes, she said we didn't DO IT enough. Most men my age, she said, are good for four or five times a week."

"FIVE times!"

"I started wondering if there was something wrong with me. But that's not the worst part. According to those tapes, there were at least a dozen common positions that we hadn't even tried. She felt cheated, I guess. Well, I did the best I could to please her, but things only got worse, not better."

"That's too bad . . . five times? Sheesh."

One Fine Evening at the Church Softball Game

By Wayne Rice

From Issue #50/August–September, 1979

"I really wanted to get our marriage back on the right track, so I picked up a book called *The Husband Book* by Dean Merrill. I thought for sure it might help. Well, he said a husband is a servant, so I started being a servant and a half. Whatever she wanted, she got. I went straight by the book."

"Did it work?"

"Ha. She read somewhere that when a husband starts acting like that, there's probably another woman."

"Was there?"

"Heck no. I assured her of that when we went to Marriage Encounter a few weeks later. And she seemed satisfied. But then they asked us to write four pages on 'How I would like my spouse to change.' I guess I shouldn't have written the part about her needing to lose weight. She's always been pretty touchy about that."

"Most women are."

"When we got home, one of our friends suggested to her that she go to a Total Woman seminar, but even that backfired. I mean, can you picture Donna standing in the doorway, all wrapped up in nothing but cellophane? I almost laughed myself sick."

"But she wasn't laughing, I take it."

"Not hardly. Look, Wayne, we really wanted a happy marriage. We read *The Act of Marriage* by LaHaye, *The Marriage Affair*, by Peterson, *The Art of Understanding Your Mate*, by Osborne, *Your Marriage: Duo or Duet*, by Evans . . . you name it, we read it. They only seemed to point out more weaknesses in our relationship, which was like the Rock of Gibraltar just a few short years ago. So the bottom line is I'm out looking for an apartment. You're up."

"What?"

"It's your turn to bat."

After I struck out, I almost recommended to Al a good book I heard about on divorce recovery, but for some reason, I decided against it.

LORD, I JUST REALLY WANT TO ASK THAT I WILL JUST REALLY BE ABLE TO JUST STOP AND REALLY QUIT USING THE WORDS "JUST" AND "REALLY" SO OFTEN IN MY PRAYERS.

From Issue #49/June–July, 1979

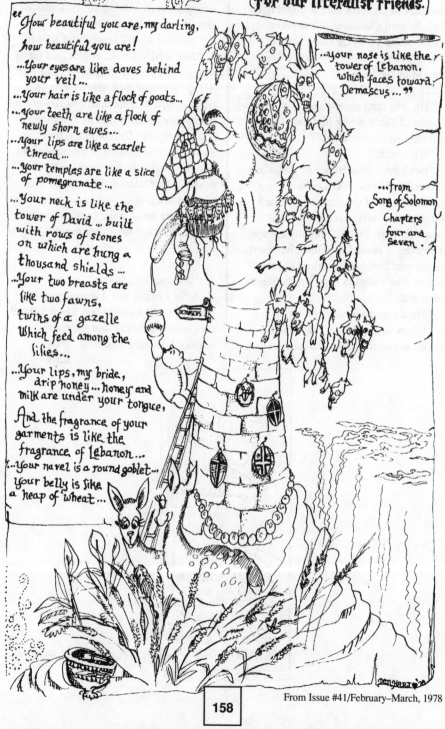

Keeping in Step With the Times

**By Dave A. Sheffel
and Tic Long**

From Issue #66/April–May, 1982

I grew up in a mildly fundamentalist home. A part of our lives was regulated by a list of taboos that became known as the Filthy Five: drinking, dancing, smoking, playing cards, and attending movies. At some point, the list was lengthened to the Nasty Nine. Then I attended a Christian college and had to sign a pledge containing at least a Dirty Dozen.

Now, as a liberated adult, I have been freed from all of those lists. I can even attend an R-rated movie and play Hearts instead of Rook. At least that's what I thought. As it turns out, now there are *new* lists. Things in the past which were simple pleasures and were free from the legalistic taboos of the narrow and bigoted have turned out to be not so simple.

Now I am told that a drive to the mountains, a long, hot shower, or putting up Christmas lights consumes too much energy. Going out to eat at a finer restaurant costs at least four times what the same meal prepared at home would cost, so I can't eat at the restaurant because I *could* give the money to the poor. Furthermore, the steaks I would eat come from beef raised in Argentina (which uses the tillable land that should be providing food for the starving in South America), and the salad is made from lettuce grown on farms

boycotted by the United Farmworkers.

However, if I drive through McDonalds to save money, then I endanger my family's health with junk food, and I support a fast-food chain which uses enough paper each year that if burned, would provide enough energy to run the city of Pittsburgh for a year. All that aside, even eating at home provides no relief because most of the processed foods I buy at the market are full of preservatives, dyes, and sugar. The fruit is sprayed with pesticides and the coffee is imported by an industry which is exploiting its workers by paying them 5 cents a day.

If I decide to escape to the television to avoid thinking about these new taboos, I end up supporting an industry that is contributing to the rapid world decline of our nation's youth and whose commercials are paid for by multi-national corporations which are raping the Third World. Besides,

159

the alpha wave radiation is negatively affecting my brain.

I don't even know where to live anymore. If I live in the suburbs, I expose my children to sub-Christian, middle-class values. If I move downtown, I raise land values and displace the urban poor. If I retreat to a monastery or commune, I isolate our family from the needy world and mitigate against the call to evangelism.

My jeans and T-shirts have labels that call my self-identity into question. My three-piece suits are worn only by power-hungry junior executives who win by intimidation, and all the leisure suits have been bought up by Southern Baptist ministers. My taxes support a militaristic government. The books and magazines I read are full of sexist language.

If I attend a conference so I can get help on what to do, there aren't enough women there, or there aren't enough blacks, or there aren't enough Chicanos, or the hotel is too fancy, the costs are so exorbitant that they exclude the poor, or

Dow Jones Chemical owns the hotel, the speakers support abortion, or they don't support abortion, they never talk about the nuclear holocaust or they always talk about the nuclear holocaust, they believe in the inerrancy of Scripture, or they don't believe in the inerrancy of Scripture.

It's an ever-expanding list. But it gets even longer if I add all the things I am *supposed* to be doing—managing my time, spending quality time with my family, developing in-depth relationships, developing community, keeping my body in shape, learning to be color-coordinated, finding out who I am, getting what I want through Amway, attending . . .

The point is, what is a fairly committed Christian with a fairly sensitive conscience and a fairly earnest desire to do the right thing supposed to do? I guess I'll just have to wait until next week and ask my evangelical cohorts while we have a beer and smoke a cigar at our weekly poker game.

From Issue #71/February–March, 1983

The Commandments of Me

DELIVERED TO MAN BY A MAN IN MARIN COUNTY

1. You shall express your feelings, no matter who gets hurt.
2. You shall grow and let nothing stand in your way.
3. You shall never let anyone tell you how to live, unless he or she is a self-actualized person who gives off positive energy.
4. You shall not criticize anyone's trip, or let yours be criticized.
5. You shall understand your basic personality makeup, and give in to it.
6. You shall allow perfect freedom of speech, unless someone is talking about religion.
7. You shall not repress your anger, but locate and express it as often as possible.
8. You shall break off all relationships when they are no longer helping you to grow.
9. You shall enjoy your sexuality whenever you feel it, which is at all times.
10. You shall never think too much about tomorrow, because who knows what kind of a person you will have grown to be by then.
11. You shall not be polite or restrain your tongue, for that would be repressing your feelings.
12. You shall criticize materialism, rigidity, and hypocrisy wherever it is found, except in yourself or in your friends.
13. You shall realize that your parents have done you great harm in the way that they have raised you, and pay them back.
14. You shall not steal, unless it is from a repressive person or institution.
15. You shall always make sure you have enough space, even if it means stiff-arming someone.
16. You shall never hurt anyone.

By Tim Stafford
From Issue #46/December, 1978–
January, 1979

TOP: From Issue #59/February–March, 1981; CENTER: From Issue #58/December, 1980–January, 1981; BOTTOM: From Issue #88/December, 1985–January, 1986

THIS CERTIFIES THAT

_____

WAS IN ATTENDANCE AT CRYSTAL EVANGELICAL FREE CHURCH

on Super Bowl Sunday evening, January 26, 1986

and is therefore designated as one of the

PASTOR'S FAVORITE PEOPLE

given at New Hope, Minnesota this 26th day of January, 1986

Millard J. Erickson

Interim Preaching Pastor

NEGLIGENCE—"Act of God" Defense, The Supreme Court of Louisiana has refused to allow application of the "Act of God" defense in a personal injury suit brought by one worshiper against another on allegations that defendant ran into plaintiff while plaintiff was in the aisle of a church praying. Defendant had contended that she was "trotting under the Spirit of the Lord" when the accident occurred. Bass v. Aetna Ins. Co., 370 So.2d 511 (opinion by Justice John A. Dixon, Jr.).

ABOVE LEFT: From Issue #52/February–March, 1980;
ABOVE: From Issue #54/April–May, 1980;
BELOW: From Issue #65/February–March, 1982

Wanda Ritchie's Evangelical Boutique DESIGNER JEANS FOR
THE WELL-DRESSED CHRISTIAN

Hal Lindsey "Late Great Jeans"
They won't come off until the rapture, or until you make a million bucks—whichever comes first.

Jimmy Bakker "PTL Jeans"
Made of flannel, with feet in them; teddy bear included.

Ronald Reagan "Presidential Jeans"
Old but expensive; faded spots dyed to look like new.

Francis Schaeffer "Knicker Jeans"
The knee length jeans who are there.

Thomas Howard "Liturgical Jeans"
Traditional styling in a variety of boring colors.

Charlie Shedd "Exciting Jeans"
Big enough to include your wife.

Lyman Coleman "Serendipity Jeans"
Fold 'em up into your view of the church.

Jim Wallis "Sojourners Jeans"
Zip up a pair and be in a bad mood.

Peter Wagner "Expanding Jeans"
They grow on you.

Mark Hatfield "Political Jeans"
They look like jeans, but they're really slacks.

Billy Graham "Crusade Jeans"
They loosen up with age.

Charles Colson "Prison Jeans"
Come in a variety of colorful stripes; ball and chain extra.

Jerry Falwell "Moral Majority Jeans"
They only have a right leg; welded zipper design prevents immoral behavior.

Oral Roberts "Miracle Jeans"
Rips and tears heal right up.

Ron Sider "Hungry Jeans"
No pockets for carrying money, car keys, wallets.

Letha Scanzoni "ERA Jeans"
Made to fit both men and women.

Robert Schuller "Crystal Jeans"
The drive-in jeans made of spun glass.

Ernest Angley "Healin Jeans"
Available only in shocking pink; fur lined.

Bill Gothard "Seminar Jeans"
You don't get the jeans; only pictures of jeans.

Keith Green "Righteous Jeans"
We give 'em away.

SEMINARY STUDENT SPECIAL!

Dallas Jeans
They come in only one size, one color, one style.

Fuller Jeans
They come with interchangeable labels.

Princeton Jeans
They stretch to fit anybody.

Union Jeans
Made from the thinnest possible fabric; you can see right through 'em.

SPECIAL CLOSE OUT!

Wittenburg Door Jeans
It takes four months to get a pair; full of flaws and emphasize all your worst features.

"PUSH 'EM BACK, PUSH 'EM BACK, WAY BACK" DEPARTMENT

(The following letter was written by the head of the English Department at Purdue University. It was sent to the head football coach.)

Dear Coach:

Remembering our discussion of your football men who were having troubles in English, I have decided to ask you, in turn, for help.

We feel that Paul Sprague, one of our most promising scholars, has a great chance for a Rhodes Scholarship, which would be a great thing for him and for Purdue. Paul has the academic record for this award, but we find that the aspirant is also required to have other excellences, and ideally should have a good record in athletics. Paul is weak physically. He tries hard, but he has troubles in athletics. But he does try hard.

We propose that you give some special consideration to Paul as a varsity player, putting him if possible in the backfield of the football team. In this way, we can show a better college record to the committee deciding on the Rhodes scholarships. We realize that Paul will be a problem on the field, but—as you have often said—cooperation between our department and yours is highly desirable, and we do expect Paul to try hard, of course. During his intervals of study, we shall coach him as much as we can. His work in the English Club and on the debate team will force him to miss many practices, but we intend to see that he carries an old football around to bounce (or whatever one does with a football) during intervals in his work. We expect Paul to show entire good will in his work for you, and though he will not be able to begin football practice till late in the season, he will finish the season with good attendance.

Sincerely,

Head, English Department

P.S.—We are delaying a decision on your request made to this department regarding a passing grade for your fullback, until we receive your favorable reply.

From Issue #24/April–May . . . June, July, August, September [circle your favorite], 1975

It's Time To
Party

By Mike Yaconelli

From Issue #105/May–June, 1989

Recently, my wife and I were having our devotions and reading our favorite devotional guide, *Cosmopolitan*. In it was another one of those mindless quizzes. (You know the ones: How Responsible Are You? How Sensual Are You? Do you Have ESP? Will Your Marriage Last?) One of the questions caught my eye. It said:

Which would you prefer?
a) a wild, turbulent life filled with joy, sorrow, passion, and adventure—intoxicating successes and stunning setbacks, or
b) a happy, secure, predictable life surrounded by many friends and family, without such wide swings of fortune and mood?

I thought the answer was obvious. Everyone, I thought, would choose the first option. I was shocked to discover that a good majority would choose the second option. And then it occurred to me: I have been working with adolescents for the past twenty-nine years. And, when I ask them

to describe adults, one word always comes up—borrrrring.

As I began to think about it, I realized that most adults I know *are* boring. They don't have fun anymore. Oh sure, get a few drinks under their belts and they act alive for awhile. But that's not what I mean. I'm talking about being and acting alive *all* the time.

The truth is that games are wasted on the young. Little kids don't know how to play games. Remember when you were seven years old and you played hide and seek? You'd hide behind a telephone pole with half your body hanging out. No, hide and seek isn't for children. It's for people like you and me. Now that I am forty-six, *I know how to hide*. I'm a darn good hider.

I have suggested a game of hide and seek to many adult audiences and I am always amazed at the response. I see adults all throughout the group nudging each other, quietly discussing a great hiding place they just thought of, secretly planning a game with their children. It doesn't take much to make most of us realize that we have become too serious, too tense, too stressful. The result is that we have forgotten how to live life. It seems like the older we get, the more difficult it is for us to enjoy living. It reminds me of a description of life given by Rabbi Edward Cohn:

"Life is tough. It takes up a lot of your time, all your weekends, and what do you get in the end of it? . . . I think that the life cycle is all backward. You should die first, get it out of the way. Then you live twenty years in an old-age home. You get kicked out when you're too young. You get a gold watch, you go to work. You work forty years until you're young enough to enjoy your retirement. You go to college; you party until you're ready for high school; you go to grade school; you become a little kid; you play. You have no responsibilities. You become a little baby; you go back into the womb; you spend your last months floating; and you finish up as a gleam in somebody's eye."

It's hard to imagine we were a gleam in someone's eye once. What happened to the gleam in our eye? What happened to that joyful, crazy, spontaneous, fun-loving spirit we once had? The childlikeness in all of us gets snuffed out over the years.

A.W. Tozer once said, "This society has put out the light in men's souls." He had it right. The more pagan a society becomes, the more boring its people become. The sign that Jesus is in our hearts, the evidence of the truth of the Gospel is . . . *we still have a light on in our souls*. We still have a gleam in our eye. We are alive, never boring, always playful, exhibiting in our everydayness the "spunk" of the Spirit.

The light in our souls is not some pious somberness. It is the spontaneous, unpredictable love of life. Christians are not just people who live godly lives. We are people who know how to *live* period. Christians are not just examples of moral purity. We are also people filled with a bold mischievousness. Christians not only know how to practice piety. We also know how to party.

I believe it's time for the party to begin.

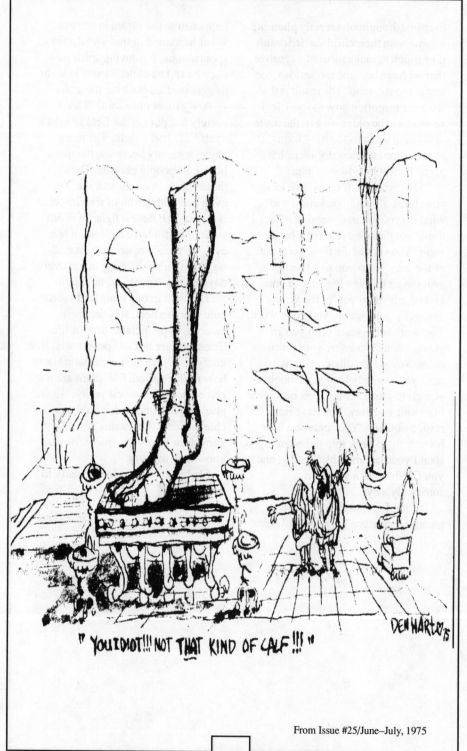

"YOU IDIOT!!! NOT THAT KIND OF CALF!!!"

From Issue #25/June–July, 1975

chase

From Issue #91/June–July, 1986

WHAT DO YOU SAY?

By Ben Patterson

From Issue #74/August–September, 1983

The nine-year-old girl was bald from the effects of chemotherapy. The psychotherapist was discussing with her the ways she could answer the questions her schoolmates would ask about her sickness. Apparently, it can be very difficult for a cancer victim of any age to explain what it feels like to be sick unto death. As I watched the videotape of their conversation over what she would say to them, I wondered also what I would say to her if I were with her. It was not the first time I had wondered over that one. I wondered about it last month as I walked into a hospital room to visit a young father of two whose kidneys were failing and who was facing a lifetime of dialysis. What would I say?

Every pastor I know has anguished over that question. I have, in the eight years I have been a pastor. And if I have learned anything, I have come to appreciate the value of saying very little. When Job's so-called friends came to visit him, they sat with him and said not a word for seven days and seven nights because they saw how great his suffering was.

That was fine. Things didn't go wrong until one of them, Eliphaz the Temanite, broke their silence and asked Job, "If someone ventures a word with you, will you be impatient? But who can keep from speaking?" A kinder, more compassionate friend would have kept from speaking, that's who. Job's sufferings had just begun when his garrulous friends arrived. On top of all of his loss was added the pain of listening to their analysis and advice.

Think of the times you have needed comfort. How much better would it have been for you if that Christian friend had just shut up instead of solemnly urging you to ponder what God must be trying to teach you through the pain! My friend was in great pain immediately after back surgery, and was asked by a Christian visitor, "What is God teaching you through all of this?" My friend winced and said through clenched teeth, "He is teaching me that it hurts like hell to have back surgery."

Or how much better would it have been if what Phil Yancey

calls that "professional cheer-leader to the sick"—who had come to see you—had just remained silent. But she chattered on and on about the weather and the children and the pennant race; anything to avoid acknowledging the sickness or hurt—as though happy thoughts and faith and trust and a sprinkling of pixie dust would make it all go away.

Certainly silence would have been more healthy to you than the exhortation you received from the television preacher. He told you that sickness was never God's will but of the Devil. He told you that if you had enough faith, God would make you well. Or if only your super-spiritual aunt had stayed silent, rather than tell you that Christ had brought this great calamity upon you so He could use you as an example of faith to others.

There is an apocryphal story about Albert Einstein, in which he was the featured speaker at a din-ner given in his honor at Swarthmore College. When it came time for him to speak, he stood up and told the astonished audience, "Ladies and gentlemen, I am very sorry, but I have nothing to say." And he sat down. A few seconds later, he stood up again and said, "In case I have some-thing to say, I will come back and say it." Six months later, he wired the president of the college with the message: "Now I have some-thing to say." Another dinner was held and Einstein made a speech.

I have rarely, if ever, had to apologize for things I have not said, but I have often had to apologize for things I did say. We live in a world in which words have become inflated. There are so many words that mean so little anymore, that words have lost their currency. Those who would heal and bring comfort to the vic-tims of evil must learn the value of silence, and of not saying any-thing unless it really needs to be said.

All of this is not to say that we should never speak a word of ad-vice or analysis to those struck down by evil. It is to say that the greatest thing we will probably ever do for them is to simply be with them in their pain and loss. At the height of the integration controversy in Alabama, a first-grade white girl went to a newly integrated school on the first day of classes. Her mother worried all day, and when her daughter came home in the afternoon, she asked her anxiously, "How did every-thing go, honey?" Her daughter answered, "Oh, mommy! You know what? A little black girl sat next to me!" Fearful of trauma of some kind, the mother tried to ask calmly, "And what happened?" Her daughter said, "We were both so scared that we held hands all day."

I'm scared when I enter a hospi-tal or home where there is great suffering. The persons suffering are scared too. What will happen to them? What can I say? How would I face it if I too were in their shoes? Will I one day be in their shoes? The monstrous powers of death and evil are so much bigger than any of us. They terrify and they intimidate. We don't need so much to explain them to each other as we do to hold on to each other and to our God when they come.

That, finally, is all God Himself assures us of in the here and now of our encounters with evil. He nowhere promises healing in the here and now. He nowhere promises understanding and comprehension in the here and now. He nowhere promises that if you do everything right and keep your nose clean that He will shield you from all evil. What He does promise is the presence of His Spirit to uphold and to comfort us. Paul calls this Spirit, the "father of compassion and the God of all comfort, who comforts us in all our troubles, so that we can comfort those in any trouble with the comfort we ourselves have received from God."

I went through what amounted to two broken engagements over a five-year period—and with the same girl. When it was all over forever and I knew it, I went to visit a close friend who had been intimately acquainted with the details of everything that had happened during that painful and stormy period of my life. I was numb and tired of hurting. We talked for a while and when I got up to leave, he suggested that we pray together. I prayed first and then waited for him to begin. Nothing came for a long time. I was about to ask what was wrong when I heard something. It was a sob. Cliff was weeping for me when I could no longer weep for myself. There have been few times in my life when I have felt as comforted. He was a little bit of the Holy Spirit to me at that moment. By the power of the same Spirit may we be the same to each other.